Saturday Night
Musings

Timely

Meditations

Connecting

Life & Scripture

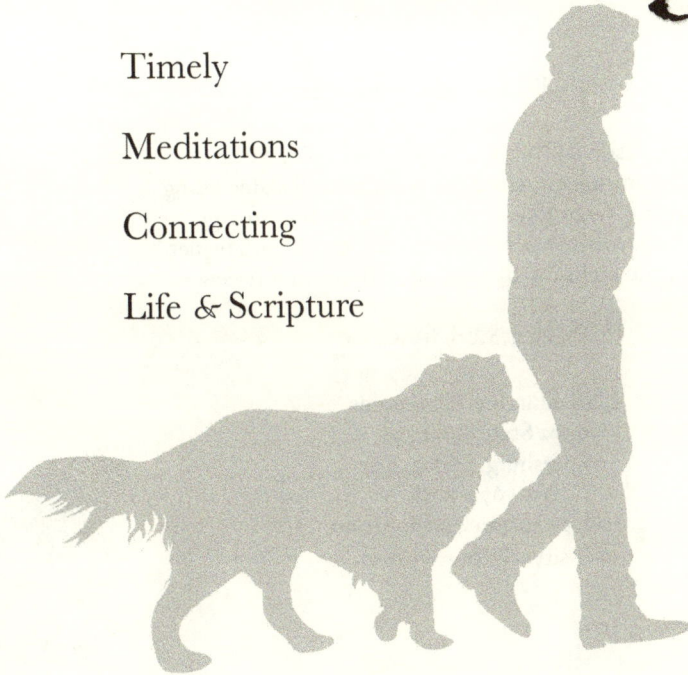

CLIFF HARTLEY
foreword by Dr. Jerry Falwell

LIBERTY
UNIVERSITY
BOOKS

Photography courtesy of Day Star Photography
Millersburg, Ohio

ISBN-13: 978-0-9819357-5-1

Cliff Hartley Ministries
6992 State Route 39
Millersburg, OH 44654
(330) 674-5709
e-mail: cwhartley@adelphia.net
website: cliffhartley.com

LIBERTY
UNIVERSITY
BOOKS

A Division of Liberty University Books
Lynchburg, VA

Dedication

First to Jeanie, a devoted wife whose value has exceeded the riches of rubies and whose love has excelled above women.

Second to Brett and Tatiana, their children, Madison and Taylor. Also, to Todd and Sue, and their children, Cara and Nathan. All of whom loves me just for who I am.

Contents

Foreword

Cliff Hartley has written an insightful collection of thought-provoking devotions entitled, *Saturday Night Musings*. These heart-moving meditations stir the soul, challenge the mind and move the heart. They have grown out of many years of pastoral ministry and expose the reader to the concerns of a pastor's heart.

I pray that you will read these meditations with an open heart and let God fill your soul with the grace of His love and the power of His Word. As you read, Cliff will take you on a journey through life that will better equip you to face the challenges of your own life. Each meditation will make a beautiful and powerful way to begin or end each day with God.

May the blessings of heaven leap off these pages and fill your heart with truth for each day of your spiritual journey.

Dr. Jerry Falwell, Founder and Chancellor
Liberty University, Lynchburg, Virginia

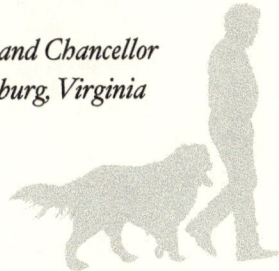

Acknowledgments

To the family and friends of the great Northside Baptist Church in Millersburg, Ohio. Because of your encouragement and persistence the Saturday Night Musings book is now a reality. Because of your love for the Lord and His Word, you have made it possible for these musings to be used in the lives of others. I know of no greater church. Thank you!

And he said unto me,
Write: for these words
are true and faithful.

REVELATION 21:5

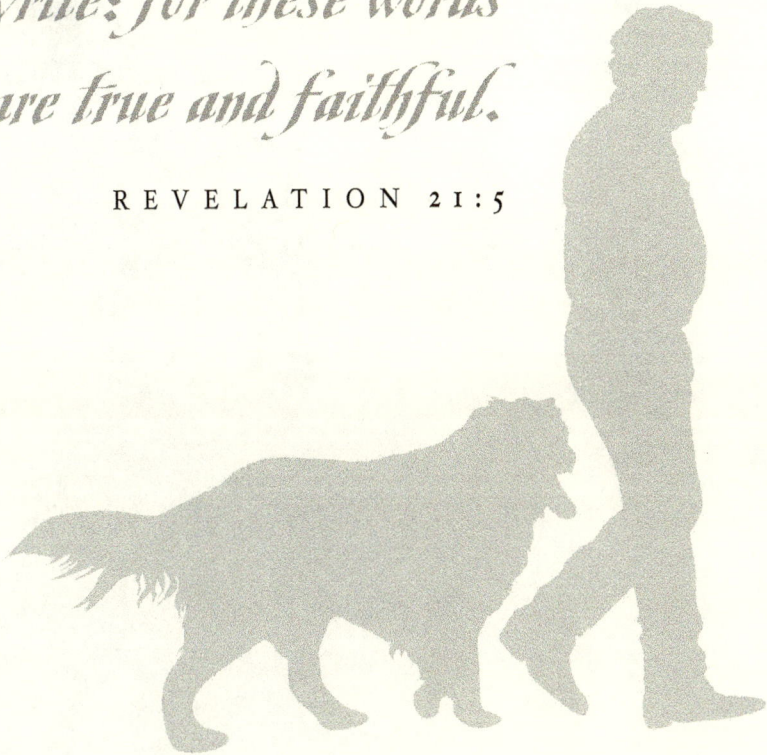

This I Do for the Gospel's Sake

I Corinthians 9:23

Do you have pretty feet? You do if you are a courier of the Gospel, the good news and glad tidings from the Lord. Our Lord is no respecter of persons and neither should we be. The Gospel is to be proclaimed to every person—every person. *How beautiful are the feet of them that preach the gospel of peace, and bring glad tidings of good things* (Romans 10:15)! The Gospel is God's message to the world about the sufferings, death, burial, and resurrection of His only begotten Son, Jesus Christ. Anyone, anywhere, anytime, who confesses with his mouth and believes in his heart that God raised Jesus from the dead can be born again, that is, S-A-V-E-D!

The Christian church can evangelize the world in a single day...if each believer would win just one person. What will it take to do that? It will take the height and the depth of our sincere spirituality. It will take nothing less than total surrender to the will of God from a selfless spirit to the Father's business. This is the will of God concerning you, me, and every child of God who has received the forgiveness of sins through the shedding of His blood, and the hope of heaven is to do whatever it takes to witness to every person that crosses our path. There are some who have never shared this good news, not even to one single person. There is not a single record in their file of ever leading anyone to Christ. I ask you, why not? We won't win every person, but if we don't try, we won't win anybody.

It is of necessity, the hour is late, and there are multitudes in the valley of decision. They are lost and

without hope in this world and the world to come. God is crying out from heaven's port, *"Who will go for us?"* There need to be those who will submit to this plea and say, *"Here am I, send me."* We are stewards of the Gospel and will stand accountable to Him one day for this ministry. *Woe is me, if I preach not the gospel.* There is nothing in this life that is as important as winning the lost to Jesus.

There is joy in heaven over one sinner that repents...and joy in the heart of the soul-winner here as well! *For if I do this willingly, I have a reward...* The laborer is worthy of his hire. God will not be a debtor to any man, and there will be a prize at the end of the race for everyone who has been in the arena for souls. The sacrifice for the Gospel's sake in this world will not be compared to the crowns won for the Master in that day. Now is our time, this is our day; we must make the most of it for the sake of others.

We are nothing more than servants of the Lord doing His bidding. If it means turning hamburgers in a fast-food place to get the Gospel out, that is what we will do. This may be humbling to the status quo, but if it is the will of God, then there is no better place to be. *To the weak became I as weak, that I might gain the weak: I am made all things to all men, that I might by all means save some.* We may not be able to go to the mission field, but can we not walk across the street and tell someone about Jesus? Someone did that for us. Return the favor to someone else.

Connect

What will we do with the incorruptible soul-winner's crown which the Lord will give for winning others to Christ? If we win that crown for the Gospel's sake, we will cast it at the feet of Jesus when we see Him face to face. Win the lost at any cost!

JUST A THOUGHT...
It may be the last time the very next person we meet will have to respond to the message of Christ.

The Glory of His Grace

Ephesians 1:6

It is just a terrific story of the Scriptures: The Queen of Sheba (unnamed) heard of the wisdom and prosperity of King Solomon in Jerusalem. She gathered a great entourage of her staff, loaded her camels with gifts of spices, gold, and precious stones for King Solomon, and came to see if what she had heard of him in her own country was true. Having seen the king, ...she said to the king, It was a true report that I heard in mine own land of thy acts and of thy wisdom. Howbeit I believed not the words, until I came, and mine eyes had seen it: and, behold, the half was not told me: thy wisdom and prosperity exceedeth the fame which I heard (I Ki. 10:6,7).

I tell you a truth, unlike any other King before Him, a greater than King Solomon is with us. He (God) has provided you and me access to Himself through Christ. Having experienced time with Him, and hearing from Him, we too are convinced that the half has not been told or could be learned of our great God. Were it not for the Scriptures, it would have never entered into our hearts the things which He has prepared for us. The end of all of this is praise for the glory of His grace by being accepted in the beloved. By coming to Him (as did the Queen of Sheba), we too can experience the ever-abundant riches of His grace which we will praise Him for all eternity.

His glory is defined by His provision of salvation to whosoever will come. This so great salvation is available for anyone who comes to Him, and that salvation will last throughout the ages to come. If there was just one

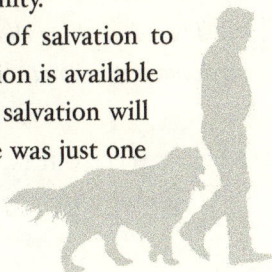

who was not able to come to Him, His glory would be less than what it could have been. For by grace are you saved through faith; and that not of yourselves: it is the gift of God (Eph. 2:8). All who do come to Him will be able to praise Him for the glory of His grace for all eternity.

The grace of God that can save from the guttermost to the uppermost is the grace that can sustain you in anything that will ever come against you. For we are his workmanship, created in Christ Jesus unto good works, which God hath before ordained that we should walk in them (Eph. 2:10). Because His grace is sufficient for any trial or testing, we can endure and enjoy life as we have it and lift up praises for the glory of His grace in every situation. If a burden is too heavy to bear, then the grace of God has failed.

It is the grace of God that enables anyone anywhere to lift up even the smallest finger pointing others to the saving grace of God. We could not do anything were it not for the effectual working of his power in us (Eph. 3:7). We would be as useless as a left-handed monkey wrench were it not for the gift of grace to serve Him. He gets all the glory!

Were it not for the grace of God speaking through us, heads would roll as we vent our frustrations with those who cross our path who may not agree with us. Our purpose in life is to build others up, not tear them down. Let all bitterness, and wrath, and anger, and clamour, and evil speaking, be put away, with all malice (Eph. 4:31).

God will shout your testimony from the housetops when the sincerity of your love for the Lord Jesus is seen and witnessed in your life to others (Eph. 6:24). Any good thing that comes from any of us, comes only by Jesus in us and the grace of God through us. If we are true men, God will never be robbed of the praise of the glory of His grace.

— *Connect* —

There is nothing that comes upon you today which God will not put in you to hold up under the most difficult testing.

JUST A THOUGHT...
God uses life's stops to prepare us for the next start.

The Woman God Gave Me
Genesis 3:12

I have known this woman as long as I have known anyone. Raised together in the same town, attended the same school and church, and became childhood sweethearts early in our adolescent and teenage years. The only girl I have ever loved has been a faithful, dedicated, and loyal wife for more than 43 years. Jeanie Compston became Mrs. Cliff Hartley about 6:40 P.M. on a Friday evening, May 18, 1963.

She told her mother when she was in the fourth grade that she was going to marry me. I told her she was endowed with a great deal of wisdom at a very early age! I said to her, "You have made a good choice." She responded at the time with, "Yes!"

The woman God gave to me has been true to her vows in marriage for 43 years. As her husband, I have no regrets, I will die with no remorse, and would do it all over again in a New York minute. Jeanie is God's gift to me every day. I am the one who is more blessed by this marriage.

The woman God gave me became the mother of two of the finest young men that I have ever known. Brett married a Christian girl (Tatiana), and they have two children, Madison and Taylor. Todd married a Christian girl (Sue), and they have two children, Cara and Nathan. These families now have Christian homes and are serving the Lord. Jeanie's influence is now in the third generation of her most prized possession— her family. Her children and grandchildren all *rise* up and *call her blessed* and rightfully so.

The woman God gave me has been my closest advisor and spiritual mentor in my ministry for more than 38

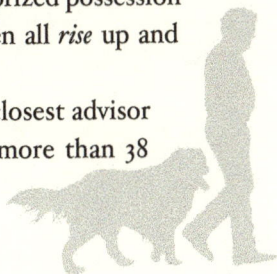

years of preaching. She is the greatest Bible teacher I have ever heard. I am much further advanced in my ministry by having her at my side. She monitors my surroundings, my associates, and my activities like a guardian angel. I am flanked on all sides by her never-ending support as the man of God who has been called to walk point as a husband, a father, and a local pastor. God gave her to me to safeguard a ministry for His glory.

The woman God gave to me has been a helpmeet in every part of my life. No other woman could have been more suitable for me than this woman. She is a Godsend and has been divinely called to give aid to the Father's business.

And the man said, The woman whom thou gavest to be with me... (Gen. 3:12). Marriage was intended for one man and one woman for a lifetime. When God made man, He made them male and female. He made a woman from Adam's rib (next to his heart) and gave her to him as a gift. He meant marriage to be heterosexual, the only arrangement which can reproduce and replenish the earth as marriage was intended to be. However, unlike Adam who blamed God for giving to him..."*that woman*", I have no blame for the woman God gave to me. I love you, Jeanie!

— *Connect* —

When the Father makes the choice for your spouse-to-be, it is a honeymoon till death.

J UST A THOUGHT...

God gave Adam a woman, not a man.

Greater Is He That Is In You...

I John 4:4

Does 14.7 pounds of pressure per square inch of your body ring a bell? We learned this in science class way back in junior high. Some 7 billion people who are alive today on this planet live under a sea of air. Scientists have estimated that for each square inch of our body, there are 14.7 pounds of pressure. For some that could be calculated anywhere from 10 to 20 tons of air pressure. Air has weight and can exert pressure. We were taught to keep the body from caving in and collapsing under such pressure. Our body counters it inwardly by pushing against the outward weight.

The evil spirit of the antichrist, the doctrine from hell, and the wickedness of the prince of this world has created an intense force against the *"little children"* (born ones) of God. The archenemy of God (Satan) has dispatched the armies of the damned to go out and cover this world with a humanistic god that can justify their willful and sensual desires. *They are of the world: therefore speak they of the world, and the world heareth them* (I John 4:5). Satan has his congregation today; they worship him and follow him.

Ye are of God, little children, and have overcome them: because greater is he that is in you, than he that is in the world (I John 4:4).

There is no pressure that can be calculated from any source which can carry an unlimited strength that can overcome even the weakest of God's children—none whatsoever! Welcome, God the Holy Spirit, who has come to take up His permanent residence in each believer. *Little*

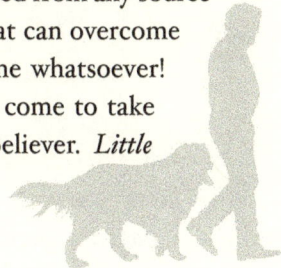

children need to let the Holy Spirit do what He came to do. Namely, to bring to your remembrance who Jesus is, all that Jesus said, and to glorify Jesus. Try this formula the next time you are being pressured by those on the outside.

He that is in you—the Spirit of truth. *You shall know the truth, and the truth shall make you free* (John 8:32). Little children, worship Jesus—God's only incarnate begotten Son who was virgin born, lived a sinless life, suffered and died to meet His Father's righteous demands, and after three days He rose from the dead to ascend back to the Father in a glorified body. Soon, and very soon, this same Jesus will come in like manner as He was seen ascending to heaven. This is the truth that will withstand any amount of pressure that can be hurled against us from the nearest corridors of hell. I can now do all things through Him that strengthens me, and I am now more than conqueror through Him that loves me. I am always in a triumphing state over sin, Satan, and hell.

He that is in the world is the spirit of error. Hello, Mr. Fool... *The fool has said in his heart there is no God.* He has been spooked, hoodwinked, blindfolded, and made a twofold child of hell. The message of the Gospel is dull to him, conforming to Jesus makes no sense, and the lust of *"his father"* is the delight of his soul. *He that is in the world* is not in Christ, and Christ is not in him.

The Holy Spirit can harness, equal, and counterbalance anything, anytime, anywhere that Satan can deceitfully muster. The Holy Spirit is the one that can build you up, hold you up, and take you up out of this world full of temptations, turmoil, and trouble.

— *Connect* —

Look for the leading of the Holy Spirit in all your activities. Search out His ways in the Scriptures to interpret your doings. Walk now in that light as HE gives it to you. The world is no match for you, the child of God who walks not in the flesh, but in the Spirit.

JUST A THOUGHT...
A person standing alone can be attacked and defeated, but two can stand back-to-back and conquer.

His Banner Over Me Was Love

Song of Solomon 2:1-7

The wife said to her husband of fifty years as they were driving home one night, *"Honey, why is it that we don't sit together in the car anymore like we used to when we were dating?"* He said to her, *"I don't know, but it's not me that has moved!"*

The ugly duckling has developed into a beautiful swan. The young black Shulammite woman has just been swept off her feet with providential love from a king in a bright and shining armor. He takes her into his most coveted room and there covers her under a cloak of safety as his most prized possession. As she is drawn near to his side, for the first time in her life she is shielded from the blistering sweat of her labor and captivated by his presence. A true love story that has an everlasting honeymoon!

This King is the Lord Jesus Christ, the Captain of our salvation, the rose of Sharon, and the lily of the valleys. He is the Son of the Highest and now has become the Shepherd of our souls. In His death He has been lifted up for all to see; in His resurrection He can draw all men unto Him. He has gotten our attention by the sweet smell of His person, which has engulfed us in the midst of darkness and death.

He called me and I said, *"Here am I."* I was lifted out of the miry clay; He put my feet on a solid rock and established my goings. I now know who I am, where I came from, and where I am going. He found me in the midst of thorns, thistles, and the barbs of sin. His love has covered a multitude of my transgressions by the cleansing of His blood.

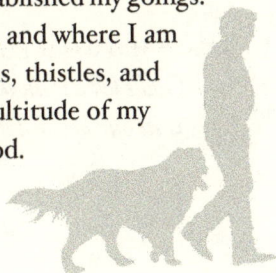

Covered by His banner of love, I now find myself sitting in His shadow with great delight, perfect contentment, and eternal assurance. There is now bread to the full, His company to enjoy, and His heartbeat to hear. It is a treasured time.

Sheltered from the weariness of labor, I now find myself dining at His table, clothed in His righteousness, and protected in His presence. It is a place of rest, a time of joy, and a way of life. My hope has surfaced and all my fears have been quieted. I'm like Peter: *"Lord, it is good for us to be here...!"*

His love for me has no equal, has no boundaries, and knows no limits. It is as if I am the only one He cares about in all this world. I am overwhelmed to the point that I have no strength but His strength, I have no desire but His desire, and have no will but His will.

His left hand is under my head, and his right hand doth embrace me (Song of Solomon 2:6). A. W. Tozer once said, *"Nearness is likeness."* It is the Father's will that I be in Him and He in me, being made into the likeness of His Son. In His hands as well as in His arms, conformance is taking place in our lives, being fashioned into the image of the Son of God.

His banner over us is His true love. My love for Him is to be single-minded, with all my heart, and for all of my life. I fear that my noise, my fleshly desires, and my worldly interest will awaken Him with my slightest movement. With this disturbance, then with a broken heart, I must say, *"Depart from me, for I am a sinful man."* Oh God, keep me near you!

— Connect —

Take this time to be holy, remove your shoes, and fall at His feet,
for you are standing on holy ground!

JUST A THOUGHT...
God's love is an unwavering commitment to what
is in our best interest, and it is given unreservedly.

I Have a Church Job

Ephesians 4:11-13

Rubbermaid in Wooster, Ohio, shut down in 2004, and 800 people had to find work elsewhere. Two hundred fifty firemen in Cleveland will lose their jobs in 2004 because of deficits in the city's budget. Corporate America has merged. They are downsizing their workforce with new technology and leaving veterans scrambling after years of service. A sad commentary which many are reading about their own destiny.

I have a church job and I have had it for more than 40 years. I have had reprimands, I have been disciplined, I have had evaluations, I have been promoted, and I have enjoyed it every day of my life. It is a job which I will never retire from, the workload will never lighten, and the pressure is ever demanding. I love my job and have never thought of doing anything else.

The CEO is God! The head of the company is Jesus Christ, the Holy Spirit is the dispatcher, and the executive offices are in heaven. It has been in business for more than 2,000 years and it is worldwide. It has ten thousand times ten thousand and thousands of thousands of servants and is always in demand for more. Millions are desperately in need of our services, the opposition is trying to shut the doors, and the laborers are few. The company I work for is the Church of God.

I have been gifted and trained to do my job. I fit the position perfectly. My job has a title of *pastor and teacher. And he gave some apostles, some prophets, some evangelists, and some pastors and teachers...* (Eph. 4). When any person becomes a believer in Jesus Christ, there is a divine gift given at the

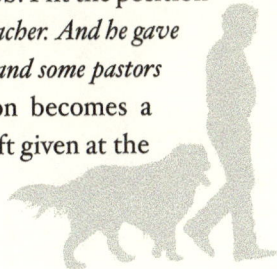

moment of salvation, equipping that person to engage in strengthening the church of God. My position is vital and it is imperative that I show up for work every day. The church was a good church before I joined it; since my coming aboard, it must get better!

My job's description is, *For the perfecting of the saints, for the work of the ministry, and for the edifying of the body of Christ.* It calls for me being a supervisor to encourage others to grow into maturity, to encourage them in ministry, and to encourage them as members in the body of Christ. I am just a helper; that is all I am and that is all I want to be. If I can just help somebody...I can lay my head down at night knowing I have done a good day's work.

And another thing about my job, I have job security. *Till we all come in the unity of the faith, and of the knowledge of the Son of God, unto a perfect man, unto the measure of the stature of the fullness of Christ.* I want to be more like Jesus and want others to be more like Jesus. One day the body of Christ will stand, having no spot, no wrinkle, and without blemish, a beautifully adorned bride.

— *Connect* —

Until that day when we all stand matured in faith, totally united in the person of Christ, and receive His fullness, we will never be out of a job and will always have work to do.

JUST A THOUGHT...
It has been said that Christ's Church is a recruiting agency for the kingdom of God (Mason).

My Sin Is Ever Before Me

Psalm 51:3

Every morning as I shave in front of the mirror, I'm reminded of what took place some 47 years ago. I have a huge scar on my left forearm that resulted from neglect, rebellion, and pride. I was told by Dad that I could not drive his plumbing truck till I had my license. It was on a rainy Sunday afternoon that I was going to show some of my buddies that I could drive a floor stick shift. I ran to my dad's truck, opened the door, slipped on the running board, and fell to the floor, crashing down on an old rusty can of pipe fittings. I ripped a gaping gash into my left arm that left a scar for God and everyone to see. Needless to say, the pain is gone and the embarrassment has passed, but that day and my scar will never let me forget my disobedience to my dad.

One of the most remembered stories in the Bible is that of David and Bathsheba. King David committed two of the most cardinal sins that can be committed: adultery and murder. He impregnated another man's wife and then had her husband (Uriah, the Hittite) killed in battle. Confession to these sins did not come till approximately a year later, when Nathan the prophet came for a visit and pointed out David's sin. The prophet told David that the sword would never depart from his house and that his sin would be published before all people and before the sun. David said, *"I have sinned against the Lord."* Nathan said to David, *"The Lord has put away your sin."* And indeed He did, yet this story of David's shame and sin will not go away. Every time he walked on the rooftop, his sin was before him. Every time there was a war, his sin was before him. Every time David loved Bathsheba, his sin was before him!

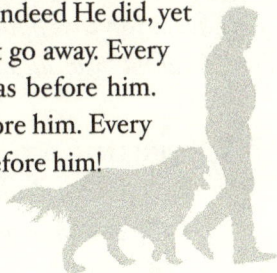

We all have a sinful past, and sin leaves an indelible stain in our lives which will never go away. Our Lord is both gracious and compassionate. He is a forgiving God that will hurl our sins into the depths of the sea (Micah 7) when they are repented of and openly confessed before Him. *Though our sins be as scarlet, they shall be white as snow; though they be red like crimson, they shall be as wool.* By the blood of Christ we now have atonement, justified by faith, and are saved eternally. Nothing in the past or in the future will abort that. Thank God for His tender mercies and great grace.

Wash me thoroughly from mine iniquity, and cleanse me from my sin. There is no sin that has been committed or can be committed that can not be washed completely and stay forever clean. We are to ask God to search our hearts to show our sin, even our secret sins and forgotten sins. Ask for His forgiveness and experience His peace.

For I acknowledge my transgressions: and my sin is ever before me. Stop blaming *Joab* or *Bathsheba* for your wrongdoings. It's not my brother or my sister, but it is me!

Against thee, thee only, have I sinned, and done this evil in thy sight. Listen to this one: *Thy word have I hid in my heart, that I might not sin against thee.* It is God who has defined what sin is. When we miss His mark, we have sinned against Him.

Create in me a clean heart, O God; and renew a right spirit within me. Though our sin will ever be before us, yet we can experience His strength, His righteousness, His power, and His grace. We will be able to experience a victorious Christian life of devoted service unto the one who has loved us with an everlasting love. Amazing Grace!

— *Connect* —

Bow your head right now and ask God to show you any secret sin which may not at this time have been openly acknowledged before Him. He knows about them all; all He is waiting for is to hear them from you.

JUST A THOUGHT...
"Sin is a clenched fist, an outstretched arm, and a mighty blow in the face of God."

Pray Without Ceasing

I Thessalonians 5:17

On July 4th weekend, over 40 million
people who live in this one fruitful and blessed
nation under God will *"hit the road,"* traveling to all sorts of
vacation resorts for some *"r and r"* with family and friends. (And rightfully
so, I might add!) To those 40 million and the other some 260 million
here at home in their fine pools and comfortable hammocks, stop
and offer prayer for the families who have lost moms, dads, sons, and
daughters in the Iraq War (not to mention those lost in Afghanistan).
According to recent reports, more than 2,500 of our troops have died
for the sake of freedom in that country and around the world. As you
and your family enjoy this freedom in America, please remember the
family of our Armed Forces in harm's way at this moment.

Our gracious, compassionate, and wonderful heavenly Father has
provided to all men direct access to Him anytime, from anywhere, and
for whatever petitions which any person might have. There has never
been a power failure that has caused delays or any interrupted service
unto His throne. We are all needy people and our God in heaven can
supply all our needs. There is not a prayer which He can not answer
and not a problem that He can not solve. His ear is always attentive and
His arm is never short of extending even to the remote parts of the
earth. *Call upon me, and I will answer you, and show you great and
mighty things which you know not* (Jer. 33:3).

With all this in mind, all of our great failures are
prayer failures. Simply put: *We have not, because we ask not.*
Someone has carefully said, *"If a man can pray, he can do*

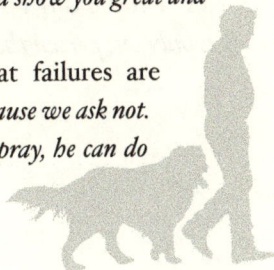

anything." And again, The effectual fervent prayer of a righteous man availeth much (James 5). The strength of our lives lies in our prayer life. Our greatest sin therefore must be prayerlessness. Prayer was the place where we were when we got started in the family of God. We confessed our sins and believed Jesus died for us. God heard that prayer and saved our souls from hell and promised us a place in heaven.

To be able to pray without ceasing is the availability of the reoccurrence of prayer...at the drop of a hat! It seems to me that if we can pray without ceasing, we can ask God and keep on asking God. Ask and it shall be given you... For everyone that asketh (keeps on asking) receiveth..." He never tires of listening to His children, so ask!

I think this is strengthened when the Scriptures say, That men ought always to pray and not to faint. Do not become weary in well doing, keep believing God, and keep going to God, ...for he that cometh to God must believe that he is, and that he is a rewarder of them that diligently seek him.

Again, Jesus said, "And all things, whatsoever ye shall ask in prayer, believing, ye shall receive." No matter what? No matter what! With this resource, why would we ever want to stop praying?

— *Connect* —

Now get hold of this verse and make it a life verse: Because he hath inclined his ear unto me, therefore will I call upon him as long as I live (Psa. 116:2). Pray as long as you live and you will pray without ceasing! So, bow your head right now...and pray!

J ust a thought...
There is only one person that can keep you from praying—that is you!

This Is My House

Joshua 24:15

Someone has said, *"Families just ain't born, you have to work at 'em, even when there ain't much to work with."* "Mother's Day"—where would we all be without our dear precious mothers? Thank you, Mothers, for all that you have done for us. We love you. John Wesley said, *"All that I am I owe to my mother."* (Suzanna Wesley, the mother of seventeen children.) Me, I'm one of eleven children (nine still living) and next to the youngest. I feel a little like what the late Robert Kennedy once said, *"I was the seventh of nine children. When you are that far down, you have to struggle to survive!"*

I read a story sometime ago from the AP of a little girl who went to a drunken romp, became pregnant, and now is an expectant mother at the age of eleven! Mr. Warren Jeffs has been arrested for having sex with a minor—one of his possible 70 wives! And recently, Liset Hernandez, 36, of Miami, Florida, was arrested with charges of one count of murder and child abuse. She said the *"demons"* told her to kill her nine-month-old baby and to stab her three-year-old daughter.

My mother would have said, "This is my house, and that is not going to happen here." Traditions for the "House that Mom built," has derived from old-fashioned biblical convictions. These convictions have "hand-me-downs" which have been proven to stand under the strongest winds of hell.

Listen to Joshua of old: *And if it seem evil unto you to serve the LORD, choose you this day whom ye will serve; whether the gods which your fathers served that were on the other side*

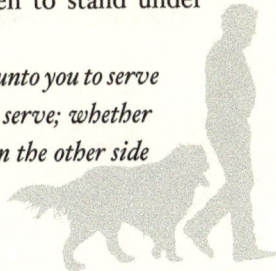

of the flood, or the gods of the Amorites, in whose land ye dwell: but as for me and my house, we will serve the LORD.

No man can serve God and the devil at the same time. You will either love one or hate the other. You can not have any graven and carved idols in your life and please the God of Abraham, Isaac, and Jacob. The God who lifted you out of the miry clay and set your feet on a solid rock is the only true God that is worthy of your love, adoration, and service. You must say, "This is my house and it will not be divided."

In every courtroom there is a judge, in every classroom there is a teacher, and in every home there is a leader. Joshua said, "...but as for me..." As Christ is the head of the church, so should the man be the head of his home. We need a few good men who stand up and say, "This is my house and we will follow the Lord."

When the tails of two tomcats are tied together and thrown over a clothesline (does anybody know what a clothesline is today?), there is union, but not unity. When husbands and wives submit themselves 100% to each other, I bet you the children in that home will submit themselves to their parents as well. Bible reading, family altars, and serving God should grace every wall, floor, ceiling, window, and door of your home. Fathers and mothers must say, "This is my house; we honor and worship the Lord here." In this, children will call their parents blessed!

— Connect —

Can we say: "That is my house"?
A place that is good, pleasant, and in harmony.

J U S T A T H O U G H T...
Anyone can build a house; it takes God to build a home.

My Church

Matthew 16:17-18

Just simply amazing, phenomenal, and 2,000 years of miracles that have been ongoing since the Holy Spirit descended to take residence upon 120 persons meeting in a room and gave birth to...*my church! My church* is the fastest growing, the oldest in history, and the greatest hindrance to the work of the devil unlike he has ever seen. *My church* was a great church before I joined it. Having joined it, I made it a better church. Since I joined it, millions upon millions have come to make it greater. One day *my church* will stand in numbers as the sand of the seas without spot, wrinkle, or blemish, having been washed and made clean through the blood of Christ. I love *my church* and do not know where I'd be today without her.

And Jesus answered and said unto him, Blessed art thou, Simon Barjona: for flesh and blood hath not revealed it unto thee, but my Father which is in heaven. And I say also unto thee, That thou art Peter, and upon this rock I will build my church; and the gates of hell shall not prevail against it.

Trust me... Peter is not the founder of *my church,* and *my church* was certainly not built upon him. Peter was a stone (a little stone) which the Lord used in *my church* as well as in others which He is using in this life-changing work that has encompassed the globe. As of this date, *my church* is still in a building program, calling out the bride made up of living stones from all over the world.

My church is built upon the chief cornerstone (the big stone), a foundation which no other man has or can lay. That stone is *the Christ, the Son of the living God.*

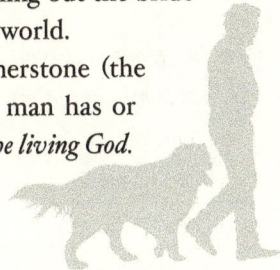

It is upon this rock (Christ), God's only begotten Son, that *my church* becomes a major force, a mighty fortress, with a message of forgiveness to whoever will accept Him.

Christ said: *I will build my church! My church* is His church. Christ will build *my church* by calling people like Peter, and James, and John, and you and me, bringing our confession that He is the Christ, the Christos, the Messiah, and all that He claims to be. Neither Higher criticism nor Gnosticism has squalled enough to silence this truth. *My church* is not built upon sand but upon that huge rock that can weather the fiercest winds of hell. The big bad wolf can huff and puff as long and as loud as he wants, but he can not blow *my church* down.

My church is a glorious work as a bride prepared for her husband. She is the *ekklesia*, the called-out ones, the ones who have turned to God from idols, immorality, and adultery. He can take the Sauls and turn them into Pauls. He can turn sinners into saints. He has taken the guttermost and used them to the uttermost. *My church* is being added to daily and being conformed unto the image of its builder.

My church is the barrier and the opponent against the thoughts and the intents of hell. This world is a better place to live because of *my church*. Neighbors are better neighbors and employees are better employees because of *my church*. So, you don't believe that? Well, just wait and see what will happen when *my church* has been removed from this world. *My church*, I love it!

Connect

My church is Christ, and Christ is my church. I am part of Him, His body, carrying out His great commission unto all the world.

JUST A THOUGHT...
What is missing in my ch_ _ch, when you do not attend? UR!

My Father's Business
Luke 2:49

Henry Ford III, at 26 years of age, has recently entered the family business. He is the second member of the fifth generation of the Ford family and the great-great-grandson of the founder of the Ford Motor Company—Henry Ford!

The world's largest retailer business is a family-run business that has more than 1.5 million employees and now is in the third generation—Wal-Mart Super Stores!

Some 35% of Fortune 500 companies are family-run businesses. These companies produce 50% of the U.S. gross domestic product. They generate 60% of the country's employment and 78% of all new job creation. (*Business Week*—February 13, 2006.)

What about a family business that has been an ongoing work for thousands of years! What business? It's *"my Father's business!"* I'm about the *999th zillion* family member of this organization. The business is open 24/7 and 365 days a year. The doors are always open for anyone and there is always room for one more to come in. This business has marketed a product that will meet everybody's need. It is a place where *"word of mouth"* is its method of advertising, and once people have come, they just keep coming back and bringing more with them. This business is *my Father's business,* and His business will put the Ford Motor Company and Wal-Mart in perspective!

"I must be about my Father's business," was said first by God's only begotten Son, Jesus—at twelve years of age. This statement is interesting, as it is the *first*

recorded saying of Jesus. The place where He said it is interesting as well—in church! Let me add this. This was said to His mother and His earthly father. The Scripture says in the next verse, *They did not understand that saying.*

When Jesus began His ministry some 18 years following His church debut, He said His coming was in the volume of the book written of Him to do the Father's will. He said, *"I must preach the kingdom of God;" "I must go through Samaria;" "I must suffer many things;" "I must be lifted up," "I must work the works which my Father gave me to do."* When He died on the cross for which He was born, the *last* thing which was recorded of Him was: *"It is finished!"*

What is the *Father's business?* It is the preaching business. But what kind of preaching? Jesus said the Spirit of God was on Him to preach the Gospel. *...it pleased God by the foolishness of preaching to save them that believe.* This is how the Father wants His business to be run. He wants preaching to be an open public discourse of the redemptive account of His only begotten Son, the Lord Jesus Christ. To the unbeliever this preaching business is foolishness, but to the "born ones," it is the power of God. *As many as received him, to them gave he power to become the sons of God.* This kind of preaching will save anyone who believes. Anybody? Anybody! When you become born again, you become a member of the *Father's family.* Once part of the Father's family and His business, the future is both secured and sealed for you.

— *Connect* —

Find out where your Father is working today and go to work.
Place your hands on the plough and do not ever look back.

J UST A THOUGHT...
Let's get busy; there is work that needs to be done!

The B-I-B-L-E, Yes, That Is the Book For Me

Psalm 119

Dan Brown's book, *The Da Vinci Code,* since 2003 has sold over 60.5 million copies and has been translated into 44 languages (Doubleday). According to Bible Society's records from 1816 to 1992, the Holy Bible has sold over 6 trillion copies of the Word of God and has been translated into 2,000 languages. One is fiction and the other is fact—go figure! THE B-I-B-L-E, yes, that is the book for me!

The Bible is totally incapable of making any mistakes even to the dotting of the *i* or the crossing of the *t*. The Bible is totally incapable of failing. Heaven and earth will pass away, but God's words will never pass way. The Bible is the only God-breathed book, divinely inspired and fully complete without any compromise, contradictions, or concision. The Bible has influenced more people than any other book—people like George Washington who said, *"It is impossible to govern the world without God or the Bible,"* and men like Patrick Henry who said, *"The Bible is worth all other books which have ever been written."* Without question, THE B-I-B-L-E, yes that is the book for me.

The longest chapter in the Bible is Psalm 119 and has the most verses in a single chapter—176 verses. And every verse in this chapter alludes to the word of God except three (84, 121, and 122)! THE B-I-B-L-E it's God's book. From Genesis 1:1 to Revelation 22:21, the Bible is God's written message to all mankind. Whosoever reads it will be blessed (Rev.

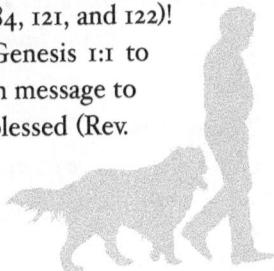

1:3), they will not be deceived, and it will guide anyone to eternal life…and that is a promise. If you pray this prayer in Psalm 119:18, *"Open thou mine eyes, that I may behold wondrous things out of thy law,"* you will be energized by the Holy Spirit as you enter into a world fully understanding the will of God. Only the Holy Spirit can break the walls of deception and can lead you into the light of God's path for all men. THE B-I-B-L-E!

There is not a person who does not sin. How to overcome sin in a dirty world is adhering to the Word of God, hiding it in your heart by memorization, and obeying it in life. When you pillow your head at night, you will have no regrets (119:9, 11). THE B-I-B-L-E!

There is not a person who does not need strength. Same as the body weakens by reason of age, the spirit needs to be revived when weakened by lust, pride, and yielding to temptation. Even Jesus was hard pressed in the Garden of Gethsemane and prayed for overcoming strength to do the will of the Father (119:28). Read THE B-I-B-L-E!

There is not a person whose songs of the homeland do not bring gladness (119:54). Songs about heaven, waiting loved ones on the other side, and the promise of going home stirs the heart unlike any merit in this world. Longing of this kind is only found in THE B-I-B-L-E.

There is not a person who does not need a shining light on a dark and dangerous path (119:105). God's Word will guide your steps and your stops accordingly. Each step I take, I take in the light of THE B-I-B-L-E.

There is not a person who has not been snubbed and offended. To keep your feelings from getting hurt, love THE B-I-B-L-E (119: 165). THE B-I-B-L-E, yes, that is the book for me. I stand alone on the Word of God, THE B-I-B-L-E!

— *Connect* —

Should there be any dust on your Bible, wipe it off with the tears of neglect and renew your God-given road map as you jump-start your journey today.

JUST A THOUGHT…

The Holy Book of the living God suffers more from its exponents today than from its opponents (Leonard Ravenhill).

This Place of Torment
Luke 16:19-31

Zacarias Moussaoui, a counterpart to the Al-Qaeda terrorist network and convicted conspirator of 9/11, will rot to death in his 7x12 concrete cell at the SuperMax Federal Prison, Colorado, known as the *Alcatraz of the Rockies*. He will live a lifelong living hell 24 hours a day without any contact with anyone. This definitive sentence is but a surface scratch description as to *the place of torment* which the Bible records about *hell*.

Hell is no joke; it is not a laughing matter. The ice is thin because of this place where the fire is not quenched and the worm never dies. All those who reject the Christ of the Bible will be turned into hell, and without any hope confined to an intense burning yet never-consuming flame.

It is the place for the dead, but where the dead never die. The rich man died, was buried, and "wham-o," he lifted up his eyes in hell, being in torments. He had all five senses up and running as well as when he lived the life style of the rich and famous. He never had a bad moment; he lived in splendor every day without ever having a need. He never had to ask for anything, he was never in want, and he never had a care in that place of ease. How quickly can the tables turn in one's life! Now in *this place of torment* he will be forever alert and will never for eternity have a good day.

The rich man said, *"I am tormented in this flame,"* this ever-devouring flame. The pain from this fire is as binding as if one were tied to a burning stake...forever. There is nothing that can kill the pain and there is nothing that

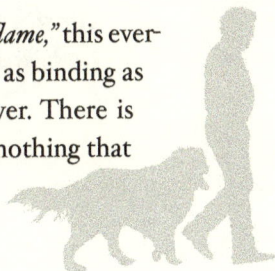

can kill the soul as one burns in an everlasting sea of fire. Nothing is so frightful as *this place of torment!*

There will never be an ounce of mercy in *that place of torment*. He cried for mercy, but only saw the bliss of the bosom of Abraham, the comforting resting place of Lazarus. Forever, the rich man will be tormented, every day, and more so as he views the heaven he could have had.

The bridge is out and it will never be repaired. Besides the *torment of the place,* in hell there is no way out of that damning hole of the abyss. The great gulf that separates the two great divides are impassable and to get to either side is now impossible. If I could I would free everyone that is in that horrible *place of torment*...but I can not. That *place of torment* will be a *place of torment* forever!

What can you do when you do not know what to do? Pray! Prayers in hell are heard, but never granted. They will go up, but the hopeful answers will never be received. The rich man prayed (he should have done a whole lot of that while on earth) for someone to witness to his family, lest they too come to *this place of torment*. Now is the time to pray, when you have assurance of having your prayers heard. Now is the time to win our families, before the sudden stop happens and the rude awakening becomes a reality.

— Connect

It seems to me there is more concern about hell from those who are in hell than there are from those who aren't (yet) in hell. Now is the time to win the lost before they are forever lost.

JUST A THOUGHT...
*The rich man now will forever lie
at heaven's gate full of torment!*

For Heaven's Sake
John 14:1-6

I remember Barbara Walters interview and documentary in December of 2005 about heaven, the afterlife, and how one gets there. She interviewed everyone from atheist to religious icons to renowned names of public view. It is interesting how the left today is defining the Holy Scriptures with their biased agenda and how they ask questions to determine what answers they want to project and to confirm.

I also remember Mr. Ronald Reagan during a debate from a platform when he said, *"I have paid for this microphone...."* I now have a platform and I want to answer some questions and make some statements about heaven...for heaven's sake!

Jesus spoke clearly about heaven and rightfully so, since He was the only one who came from heaven and returned as well. He said, *"Let not your heart be troubled: ye believe in God, believe also in me. In my Father's house are many mansions: if it were not so, I would have told you. I go to prepare a place for you. And if I go and prepare a place for you, I will come again, and receive you unto myself; that where I am, there ye may be also."* Jesus is both the wisdom of God and the Word of God. Jesus believed and taught that heaven is a real place for real people.

Heaven in the Bible can be described as a country, a garden, a kingdom, or as paradise. But I like how Jesus described it as *"My Father's house."* The place where there are many dwelling places for the entire family of God. When this life is over for we who are the born ones, the members of His family by way of new birth, we

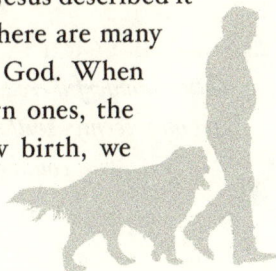

will go home to be with our Father in those mansions He has been preparing for 2,000 years.

Just where is heaven, some may ask? Heaven is up! When Jesus ascended back to the Father's right hand, He went up, and the clouds received Him out of their sight. It now is common and proper to say when people die, *"They went up to heaven."*

Who lives in heaven? Since it is the Father's house, all of the Father's children live there. I believe angels are in heaven, the Bible records about animals living there, and it is also the place where the Godhead resides. Take heart—it is not where the devil lives or any of his cronies. God has a special place for that crowd and it is not up!

When will God's children go to heaven? It seems to me that it will be at either death or as the Scriptures teach, at the rapture—the catching away of all saints. When Jesus returns, the dead in Christ will rise first, then we who are alive will be caught up in the clouds to meet Him in the air (I Thess. 4:13-18).

Will everyone go to heaven? No, only those who know the way, and the only way is Jesus. No person will get into heaven except only through Christ, who is the door. Those who have placed their trust in the crucified and risen Christ will have a guaranteed place in heaven one day, one eternal day.

Why is there a heaven? Because there is a devil and a hell. Jesus said, *"If it were not so, I would have told you."*

— *Connect* —

This is not my home, I'm just passing through. My home is laid up somewhere beyond the blue. Somehow, I'm feeling a little homesick today.

J UST A THOUGHT...
This wonderful creation of God is our home in this time, yet our eternity will be spent in splendor which we never could even begin to imagine

That Dragon, That Serpent, That Devil, That Satan

Revelation 12:9

The President of Iran is deceived. He believes the Zionist regime is acting like Hitler and should be wiped off the face of the earth. This anti-Semitic lives in this world, and he like millions has been deceived by the author of deception: That dragon, that serpent, that devil, and that Satan which has misled the whole world since the beginning of man. Over a billion of our Muslim friends have been deceived by the false prophet Muhammad. Jeane Dixon (now deceased), the psychic and astrologer, deceived America into believing the Russians would beat us to the moon and there would be a cure for cancer.

Beware of that dragon who wants to devour you, beware of that old serpent who wants to deceive you, beware of that devil who wants to distort the very Word of God, and beware of that Satan who in the end wants to destroy you and seven billion people just like you and me in hell one eternal day.

Satan is the murderous regime (*that dragon*) that has leveled his fury against God and all that God is and loves. He is the source of deception by thinking he could be like God, act like God, exalt his throne above God, and have the worship as God. This got him booted out of heaven in short order along with one third of the angels who followed his tomfoolery tactics. He landed right smack-dab in a perfect environment with perfect people, and he brought the downfall of the human race. He deceived the entire world by

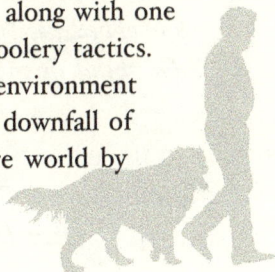

getting Eve (the mother of all living) to question what God said. *And he said unto the woman, Yea, hath God said, Ye shall not eat of every tree of the garden?* Satan is not primarily interested in taking joy in our sins, but he glories in getting you and me to believe God didn't really mean or say what He said. He is that *old serpent* and still up to his old tricks—like, *"God is too good to create a hell and send people there."* And another: *"Even if you do go to hell, you will be there with your friends."* Friend, and tell your friends, be not of that crowd which will believe a lie (he is the father of lies) and be damned. This glorious, most wise, perfect in beauty, and ever-deceiving creature of God will lead you to believe God is not all you need. You need Darwinism, you need Communism, and you need authoritarianism. He will tell you, "Go ahead, you can lift yourself by your own bootstraps!" Stupid Charlie Brown.

If you are the Son of God, command these rocks to be turned into bread. Satan will do a character assassination on you in a moment of time. He will destroy your faith, and your journey in this life will be filled with doubts and fears. The Master's meat is to do the will of the Father, not by bread alone. God is able to feed you with a cruse of oil from a widow's hand, cause water to come out of a rock in a desert, and feed you and your buddies into the thousands with a few loaves and fishes. A man's life is not in the abundance of worldly wealth. *That devil* likes to quote Scripture—if he is able to put his spin on it when he says, *"It is written...."* Jesus can quote Scripture too. As matter of fact, HE is the Scripture, and He says, *"It is written again, Thou shalt not tempt the Lord thy God."* If you know Christ, the truth, He will set you free. Satan does not know the truth, and he is not free.

— *Connect* —

That Satan can kill you! He is our adversary, and as a roaring lion he is seeking whom he may devour. His plan is to make unbelievers a twofold child of hell, deceiving them all the way to the abyss.
Go ahead, listen to this liar and see what you get.

JUST A THOUGHT...
Hide the Word of God in your heart and use it when...
that devil comes behind you.

The Coming of the Son of Man

Matthew 24:32-44

A greater than General Douglas MacArthur is here. General MacArthur's famous one-liner, *"I shall return,"* has been etched in our minds. He said this when he was captured in the Philippines during WWII. Two years later he did return, dealing a stunning victory. The greater is the Captain of our salvation, Jesus Christ, who also left us with an indelible promise: *"And if I go...I will come again..."* Two angels were dispatched from heaven and confirmed what Jesus said, as a cloud received Him out of the disciples' sight, by saying, *"This same Jesus...shall so come in like manner as ye have seen him go into heaven."* This truth of *the coming of the Son of man* was addressed to the Thessalonians, when Paul stated, *"The Lord himself shall descend from heaven with a shout..."*

Neither I nor any other man know the day or the hour when Jesus will come again, but this I do know, we are 24 hours closer to His coming than we were yesterday. Yet, there are those who say, *"Where is the promise of His coming?"* These will go on *eating and drinking, marrying and giving in marriage*, and will not know of it until it is too late. That day has now come, everything is now in place and ready for *the coming of the Son of man*. Israel is getting ready, the church is getting ready, the nations are getting ready, the rebuilding of the temple is getting ready, the antichrist is getting ready, Armageddon is getting ready, and Jesus is ready. Question: Are you ready? I hope so.

Learn the lesson of the fig tree with tender branches and full of leaves. The budding of the fig tree tells us summer is near: a time of refreshment, enjoyment, and fulfillment. This is a picture of Israel experiencing a

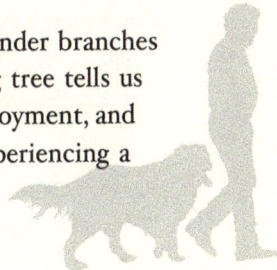

time of hope, peace, and being back home. The fig tree took root on May 14, 1948, when she was declared statehood, having rights to exist as a free country. The bones were joined together with the sinew (muscle) covering them and maturity has developed them into a strong country. We today have witnessed this generation as she has prophetically come to pass. It seems to me having this in place, *the coming of the Son of man* is near, even at the doors!

With summer here, there is one thing sure, winter is coming soon. *The coming of the Son of man* will be as when the worldwide flood took place and swept the entire human race away, except Noah and his family who entered safely into the ark. There is coming a time for Israel known as *Jacob's trouble* and the great tribulation. With the church being caught away to meet the Lord in the air, this world will enter a time of chaos and calamity of worldwide catastrophic proportions. *The coming of the Son of man* will happen when men are listening more to their career, their investments, and their retirement than looking and living for *the coming of the Son of man*.

Christ as a thief! That is—*the coming of the Son of man* will be as a thief. But know this, the Son of man will come suddenly and unexpectedly in a day and an hour when men think not. Therefore, get prepared, watch, remain faithful, and be ready. Christ will surely return as He said He would. If you are a *goodman*, set your house in order and get your family ready. As Noah's family, are all of them safe in the Ark (Christ?) Do you see in these days of plenty, clouds of darkness, discouragement, and death? Can you say, *"Even so, come, Lord Jesus"?* This is the *"terminal generation"* when we shall see *the coming of the Son of man*. Look up, *for your redemption draweth nigh!*

— *Connect* —

Prepare yourself by living by faith, giving God glory
for all things, serving in the area where God has called you,
and telling someone about JESUS today.

JUST A THOUGHT...
None of us have a promise of tomorrow.

My Last Stand Before
II Corinthians 5:10,11

You and I as believers in Christ by grace through faith in His shed blood can only be in one of two places, either on this earth or in heaven. To be absent from the body is to be present (immediately) with Him. Until this earthly house is dissolved and mortality has been clothed with immortality and this corruption has put on incorruption, we do always groan and we are always burdened, but we are always confident that when time changes into eternity for us, we will be present with the Lord.

Let the furnaces of fire, the den of lions, or even Nero's ax come. At these times, He will give us sustaining grace to stand just like He gave us saving grace which will enable us to have dying grace when it comes time to be present with Him. Take and make your stand count for God. He will go with you through these trying times.

Knowing the brevity of life, it goes without saying that there is no guarantee of the next breath; therefore, we should be in preparation for that day when we shall make our *last stand before* the judgment seat of Christ. It will be at that *"bema,"* that elevated seat where we all (saved/born ones) will stand to receive the things (rewards) done in our body, whether good or bad. You and I may not always be looking for His coming, but we will one day make our *last stand before* Him. It is an appointment where there will be no absenteeism. It could happen any moment, even at the twinkling of an eye.

Standing before Him with a record of handling hardships with all grace, forbearance, and love will be the result of hard work. *Wherefore we labor...* Enduring

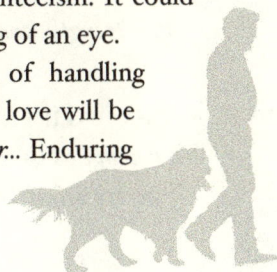

difficulties or facing discouragements is one of faith if we are pleasing in His sight. Life is not always fair; there are times when bad things will happen to good people. We will not be ready to face Him on His throne having been sissies, crybabies, or lazy used-to-bes. Quibbling must stop, quarreling must stop, and quitting must never be named among us. Life in the kingdom is hard work, 24/7, filled with thorns, and often bitter with many tears, but He always causes us to triumph for His name's sake.

How will the ministry which has been entrusted to my care measure up on that day when I make *my last stand before* the judge of all the earth? Will there be those who will be there because I have led them to Christ? Will there be a record of homes being restored because I cared enough to spend many midnight hours praying with them? Will there be those who have entered the ministry because of my ministry? He has given to me the ministry of reconciliation—that is to bring back with mended wounds and stronger bones. When I make *my last stand before* Him, what will His judgment be on how well I managed my ministry? *"A good and faithful servant?"* I can only hope so!

This will be the bottom line on that day when I make *my last stand before* Him: Did I give all glory to God for whatever I have done in His name? *Now then we are ambassadors for Christ, as though God did beseech you by us...* It is God working in us both to do His will and His good pleasure. We have nothing to glory in but to give all glory to Him for His working through us.

Connect

At my last stand before Him, I will cast crowns won at His feet and say with a loud voice, "Worthy is the Lamb that was slain to receive power, and riches, and wisdom, and strength, and honor, and glory, and blessing."

JUST A THOUGHT...

What will be His remarks when I make my last stand before Him? "Well done?" I can only hope so!

Crossing All Barriers

Acts 1:8

Taking Jesus...unto the uttermost part of the earth, is the supreme, never-ending task of the church at large today. In this day, there are many nations, ethnic groups, tribes, cultures, and hundreds of different languages. People which have never been seen or heard of are hidden on this remarkable planet. Some seven billion of *"us"* live on this beautiful earth suspended in space.

God so loved the world that he gave his only begotten Son so that all people everywhere might know Him. God crossed a unimaginable barrier by carrying out the drafted plan which ultimately brought the brutal slaying and death of Christ for the purpose of redeeming the elite as well as the heathen everywhere.

The fact that God moved and sent His Son is the explicit example of what is not being done so much today. God moved out of His domain and went to the regions beyond, crossing any and all barriers to reach the masses. Being impossible for a world which is in decay, darkness, and death to return to Him, it was God who went after them in their totally depraved state. It is not making bad people good, it is making the dead to live again. This one message now has been crossing all kinds of barriers for 2,000 years—that is, to reveal Jesus as the Savior of the world. *"Blessed Savior, Thou wilt guide us to that blissful shore."*

Missions: is the heart of God. He is not out to change the world, He is out to reach the world with the Gospel: the sufferings, the death, the burial, and the resurrection

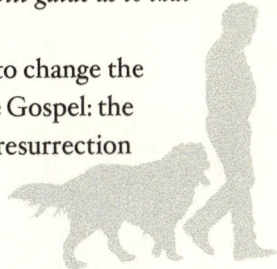

of Jesus Christ. Social programs will indeed put new clothes on an old man, but belief in the Gospel will put a new man in old clothes. What will it profit if men can claim all the wealth in this world and in the end their eternal soul perishes in the dark, heated corridors of hell? God's utmost desire is that all the world knows Jesus in the pardoning of their sin of unbelief. He will cross any barrier and reach any culture for this one purpose.

Missions: is the hope of the world. The *road map* to peace does not go through the Middle East, but rather through the heart of God. Wars and rumors of wars are part of the landscape everywhere. As long as the heart of man is bent on excluding God, His book, and His way, there will be no peace in the East or the West. There is hope today, and there is no barrier in this life which is impassable.

Missions: is the help for people. "*Ye shall be witnesses.*" The Holy Spirit, who hovers over the untouched caverns and ravines of this globe, empowers, energizes, and equips people to cross any barrier to reach any people. People like the apostle Paul, who was once a God hater and became a God lover. People like you and me, who must be willing to get up, move out, and cross any line of the regions beyond with the Gospel.

— *Connect* —

You and I are now at the end of the world. We are as far to the extreme borders of this planet as we can be without floating in space. Our mission field is next door, across the street, or that person sitting in the next chair. They are within reach and hearing distance.

JUST A THOUGHT...
You need to be winsome to win some to Christ.

Choose Life...
Deuteronomy 30:19

Rumaisa Rahman, a little Indian infant, *discovered America* on September 19, 2004, weighing in at...(are you ready for this?) 8.6 ounces! She was born 15 weeks before her arrival due date and was the size of a soft drink can. Her mother said, *"It's a blessing, it's a blessing."* She is the smallest surviving infant born on record in America. God bless this little girl for the length of days.

At the time of conception, two miraculous things take place which can never be rescinded: the beginning of a human life and the beginning of a mother. A mother has the power to stop a beating heart (18 days after conception) or to continue the pregnancy. Abortion is never the answer according to the baby.

The Hippocratic Oath in essence says that doctors will not play God in the taking of a life, but only to preserve life. Doctors have no place in the practice of medicine using their skills in the taking of a baby's life and terminating a pregnancy by the performance of an abortion. Abortion is never the alternative.

Heaven and earth record and give witness to this atrocity both now and in a day forthcoming when the hearts of all men will be judged. *I call heaven and earth to record this day against you, that I have set before you life and death, blessing and cursing: therefore choose life, that both thou and thy seed may live...* Choose life now—life which is the fulfillment of being the recipient of the blessings of God by being obedient to Him. Abortion is never an addition, only a curse!

To choose life is to choose God's way. He alone is the giver and the sustainer of life. Even in the matter of rape or incest, God is the giver of life. He takes no pleasure even in the death of the wicked. When there is life, there is always hope. Every day we live is a gift from God. Life, however it happens, is a life that has an opportunity of pleasing God. Abortion never has God's approval.

To choose life is the alternative of living a life pure from the sin of abortion, a sin which should never be once named among us. To stand guiltless before God in this matter is a quiet and comforting state. However, there is our God in heaven who forgives. The blood of His only begotten Son can clean the vilest of sinners. Though one's sins be as scarlet or like crimson, they can be washed in His blood. Abortion is never an act of innocence.

To choose life is always good for both mother and child. The relationship between a mother and a child is both cherished and treasured. One of which barren women only dream of. She has the opportunity of changing the world through this child, and this child has the opportunity of carrying out her legacy in obedience to the fourth and fifth generation. Abortion never achieves any dreams.

To choose life is to choose becoming a vessel meet for the Master's use. God can only use what you give to Him. God uses mothers in ways like no other! Abortion never accomplishes God's will.

— *Connect* —

Pray for America and nations around this world who are murdering thousands of babies every hour by way of abortion. People like you and me must stand up for those who are falling.

JUST A THOUGHT...
Wherever a human exists, there is opportunity to do kindness.

Blessed Are the Peacemakers

Psalm 120

How is a Christian to live for God in a world that is diametrically against Him and His Word? The hostility and anger that is rising from *empty minds* to eliminate God from all phases of life is on tract to produce an amoral society. A generation which knows not God may be history reproducing itself again.

U.S. Federal Judge Phyllis Hamilton of San Francisco ruled against the law banning partial birth abortion as being unconstitutional, which Congress recently passed and President Bush signed into law. The brutal crushing of a living baby's skull and extracting the brains before the baby is removed from its mother is a ruthless murder in the first degree. We must have an uprising today unequal to any in the past of saying, "Enough is enough."

These are distressful times which we are living in today. *Let not your heart be troubled.* When facing troubled times, the people of God fall on their knees in prayer. The Psalmist cried and said, "*In my distress I cried unto the Lord, and he heard me.*" The children of God are peacemakers, not troublemakers. Christians are not the ones who are troubling this nation. The Ahabs are the lawmakers, and lawbreakers are the hurtful ones. What we can do, we must do. What we can do is to pray unto God to forgive our sin and heal our land.

They have lying lips and a deceitful tongue. Blowing up abortion clinics is not the answer for these predators of innocent infants. While we take a strong stand against sin, we as children of God love the sinner. Evil for evil

is not God's way. Compassion lives in the heart of God. Forbearance can tolerate any given hate crime for a time. Vengeance belongs to God, and in the last day, God and His ways will be exonerated. These *lying lips* will one day confess that God is God.

These are the days when the tares and wheat are growing together, the pro-life and the pro-choice. We dwell in a world where peace is hated with a passion versus where the absence of peace leaves a war-riveted wasteland. Both will be uprooted someday and will be separated for eternity. Until then, the peacemakers are both salt and light, a voice crying in the wilderness to a crooked and perverse world. Where would this country be were it not for the peacemakers? The devil is hamstrung with his work by peacemakers.

Psalm 120:7: *I am for peace, but when I speak, they are for war.* There is a time for war and a time for peace. There is blood in the water today. Peace is the only answer during a bloodbath and destruction. There must be a viable voice to speak today in clear terms for the unborn and innocent lives everywhere. At the table, peacemakers are the ones who have God's ear and are spokespersons for others to live a quiet and peaceful life. The greatest peacemaker is God's only begotten Son, who bridged a gap that was ripped apart because of sin. His life is now both a legacy and a standard, which will bring the distorted out of tombs and establish them with reasonable minds. He can indeed make a peacemaker out of a lawbreaker who can champion a cause.

—Connect—

God is looking for a man to stand in the gap which will marshal a cause and provide answers to a very troubling land.

JUST A THOUGHT...
*Some are for peace, a piece of this and a piece of that.
When one learns how to spell peace, he will pursue it for himself and all that is around him. It makes all the difference in this world.*

Fishers of Men

Matthew 4:18-20

I was fishing off the shores of Jacksonville, Florida, on a boat where about 20 fishermen were on board. We were doing some deep-sea fishing. I had no idea where I was, what I was doing, or how I was doing. The captain of the fishing trip saw my dilemma and asked me to get to the rear end of the boat—out of the way of the others!

Some kind fisherman showed me how to cast my line after the "chum" had been thrown over on the other side. Little did I know that the other fishermen were doing the same thing. After some time, something hit my line (It must have been the great fish that swallowed Jonah—brother, it was a big one!) and went to the north end of the boat and then decided to come back south. When that happened, every fisherman's line was now circled and knotted together with my line. Those men were ready to throw me overboard!

Patience and perseverance saved the day. After overcoming my embarrassment and learning how to fish, I became a better fisherman by the end of the day.

Jesus said, *"Follow me and I will make you fishers of men."* Those who heard, left their boats and their nets, and immediately followed Him. They lived with Him, they loved Him, and they learned from this fisherman. Fishing for fish is somewhat like fishing for men. There are encounters that must be overcome if one is to catch men for Christ.

Fishers of men became fishers for men as they followed Jesus. Jesus left Judea and went through Samaria unto the city

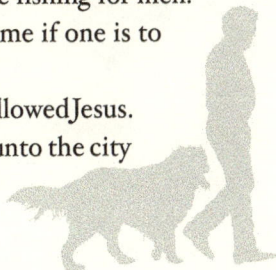

of Sychar (John 4), where He would win a Samaritan woman. John said *"...he must go through Samaria."* In the city of Sychar, Jesus would encounter a soul-winning experience with a person that others would not give the time of day. She came to draw water from the well and went home with the water of life springing up in her soul. She gave her testimony to the men of the city and many of them came and believed on Christ.

To fish for men, you must at times travel a great distance to catch them. Jesus walked some 30-40 miles to Sychar. Forget the clock, anytime is soul-winning time. Watch your line, Satan will try to get it all tangled up. This woman wanted to talk religion; Jesus wanted to talk salvation. Don't let the fish off the hook; Satan will try to knot up your fishing line. And remember this: God loves all children—red, yellow, black, and white; they are all precious in His sight. The people others will reject are people for whom His Son would die for. This woman received the water of life, and she would never thirst again. She became the soul-winner for her own town. She herself became a fisher for men. Many came to see, hear, and believe because of the soul-winning woman from Sychar.

—Connect—

Everything in water is not fish, but all fish are in water.
To fish for men, you and I have to go where the men are.

JUST A THOUGHT...
To relive the joy of your salvation is by winning others to Christ.

"For This Child I Prayed"

I Samuel 1:27

John Wesley once said, *"All that I am, I owe to my mother!"* John Wesley was the 15th of 17 children born to Samuel and Suzanna Wesley. In this day of abortion, he most likely would not have made it and the world would have missed the great Methodist Movement of John Wesley.

Mother's Day is a special day to honor and remember our mothers and rightfully so. Telephone companies tell us more calls are made on this day than any other day of the year—a day we recognize the one who gave birth to us so that we might say, *"I love you, Mom!"*

My mother (Minnie Hartley, 1908-1996) was a "stay-at-home mom" who gave birth to 11 children. A wife of one man for 45 years. She only had an eighth grade education, but you would think she carried a 4.0 toward a Ph.D. She was a cook, seamstress, secretary, teacher, doctor, nurse, bus driver, plumber, carpenter, counselor, mentor, and a Christian. She was all of the above in the course of a 16-hour workday. The last one to go to bed and the first one to rise—my mom!

The Bible speaks much about mothers. One of my favorite is that of Hannah. God opened her womb and gave her a son, whom she named Samuel. She said, *"For this child I prayed..."* (I Sam 1:27). Samuel grew into a man of God who became a prophet, priest, and a judge. No man in the Bible was more godly than Samuel. What he was and what he became, he owed to his mother.

Hannah prayed for this child: *"Lord, if you will give me a child, I will give him back to you."* He did and she did. He became all that a man can be for God all the days of his life.

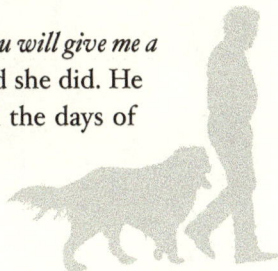

God gave this child to Hannah. Hannah had heaven's gift resting upon her breast, sitting at her knee, feeding from her table, secured under her roof, and learning from her life. She trained him daily in the ways of the Lord—and as he grew, he did not depart from the truth. The Word of God was channeled into his heart by a God-fearing mother.

Hannah gave this child to the Lord. Parents today are giving their children to everything but the Lord. Many do not pray with them or for them; they don't send them to church or take them to church. They don't know their Bible and therefore can not teach the Scriptures to their children. Hillary's book, *It Takes a Village,* needs to be replaced with the Bible. The rod has been spared long enough and the kids have been spoiled too long. Mothers must know how to get on their knees and pray for their children. Mothers must continually ask for a hedge of protection covering their children. Mothers must not allow the devil to run their house. Mothers must get their children saved, love them no matter what, and forgive them when they fail. Mothers must be a *"So help me, Hannah"* and get serious about what is serious to God—*this child!*

Connect

A mother's vow: To be a godly and praying mother.

JUST A THOUGHT…
Kids have to be straightened out or they will be hell-bent.

My Story for His Glory

Acts 9:1-9

Reports show *Martha Stewart* lied, then changed her story, which led to her downfall with a conviction and a prison sentence. *Scott Peterson's* story concerning the death of his wife, Lacy, and their unborn son have had conflicting issues. *Kobe Bryant's* story had one side, but there was another side to be told. Stories, we all have them, but few give way to the glory of God.

The greatest story ever told is that of Jesus Christ, God's Son, conceived of the Holy Spirit and born of a virgin, lived a sinless life, suffered and died on a criminal's cross, was buried in a borrowed tomb, and rose from the dead after three days. He ascended back to glory and will soon return to gather all who have trusted in Him by way of repentance of sin. Hallelujah, what a story!

When a person is in Christ, he is a new creature, old things have passed away, and all things immediately have become new. His life takes on new meaning and is radically changed. Then for a lifetime, a conformance to the Son of God takes place in us.

Consider the story of the conversion of the apostle Paul. Three times in Scripture he gives his testimony with resounding evidence of a change. Traveling on the Damascus Road, he went seeking to arrest, to persecute, to place in prison, and to slaughter Christians who were in *the way*. After being convicted and stricken to the ground, he was made known that his sin was against Jesus. From a persecutor of Christians to a preacher of the Gospel in a matter of days: *Amazing*

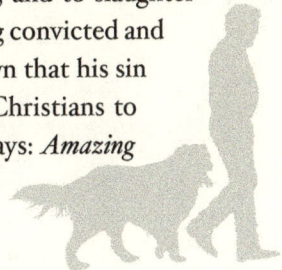

Grace! He became a chosen vessel of the Lord, suffered greatly for the name of the Lord, and served the Lord until he faced Nero's ax and died for the Lord.

What is your story? You do have one; we all do. Is it for God's glory? Do you remember a time and a place in your life when you realized it was your sin that nailed Christ to a cross. Mel Gibson's film, *The Passion of the Christ,* made you feel like you were there with Him as He took every faltering step. It also made you feel like you were the reason why He was there taking every step for you. When this truth sets in, there is a burning desire to tell your story, how He saved you from a life of hell to a life of hope and heaven.

One does not have to ride on a mule and travel on the Damascus Road to be saved. But, one does have a story of a drastic change, if indeed a change did occur. Dogs, hogs, and goats wallow in the mire and love it. However, when a man is in Christ, the chains of sin have been broken, he is at peace with his God, he is found in his right mind, fully clothed, and with a strong desire to tell his story. He may not always be what he should be, but he is not what he used to be.

"I love to tell the story of unseen things above, of Jesus and His glory, of Jesus and His love. I love to tell the story, because I know 'tis true; It satisfies my longings as nothing else can do. I love to tell the story, 'twill be my theme in glory, To tell the old, old story of Jesus and His love." That's my story and I'm sticking to it!

Connect

True conversion brings about a turning to God and a turning from sin.

JUST A THOUGHT...
"But such were some of you."

Growing in the Word of God

Ephesians 4:14

Do you remember being a youngster standing by a wall or a door with a measuring stick on the top of your head, seeing how tall you were growing? What a feeling *growing up* was like in those days! Oh, what sadness there was when growth didn't happen and there were no new marks on the wall. It is a natural desire to grow.

Physically, we stop growing taller (some, like me, are still growing wider!); spiritually, we should never stop growing. There are no limits to this. We are to *grow up in him in all things.* The moment we stop growing in Him, we become immature, and like children, we become easy prey and targets for the devil. *He is seeking whom he may devour.* One may be strong in soul-winning and weak in Bible study. Samson was strong in body, yet weak in spirit and in the will of God. It led to his downfall. The little foxes will keep many from finishing well.

That we henceforth be no more children, tossed to and fro... I believe there are *"babes in Christ"* who never grow up in Christ. These are people who have been saved a long time, they are still on milk, and they act like selfish children. *Growing in the Word of God* means one begins to develop by digesting the meat of God's Word. He meditates on it day and night, he memorizes it and hides it away in his heart, and it becomes a measuring stick for serving God. The scholar becomes the teacher and the disciple becomes the soul-winner. The "pacifiers, diapers, and bibs" become embarrassing if still lying around. Mark this down, if you get your

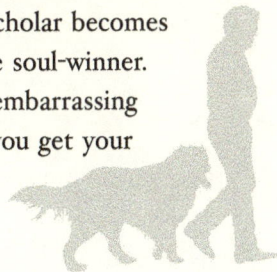

feelings hurt in certain areas of your spiritual life, it is most likely because you are weak in those spots where the Word does not control you. Listen to this: *Great peace have they which love thy law: and nothing shall offend them* (Psa. 119:165). The Word of God will make a man out of you!

...and carried about with every wind of doctrine by the sleight of men and cunning craftiness... These are the "*profits* of the gospel," and they are ravening wolves not sparing the flock. Their doctrine has no dogma, they fill their own bellies, and they are leaders of the blind, making them a twofold child of hell.

...whereby they lie in wait to deceive. Friend, they are out there in the bushes, ready for ambush, and they are taking no prisoners. All that goes on today in the name of God is not as pure as the driven fresh snow. When one is growing in the Word of God, he is *reading the Word, meditating on the Word, and obeying the Word* (Dr. C. Sumner Wemp). All else is vain jangling and a tinkling cymbal.

In the Word of God, you will read that God loves you no matter what. You will discover God's plan for your life and that He wants to include you in His program. You will find there can be real peace of having your sins forgiven with the assurance of going to heaven one day. And you will try to win others to Christ, so they can go to heaven too.

— *Connect* —————

Grow in the Word of God; it will unfit you for the devil's pundits.

J U S T   A   T H O U G H T...
Now just look at you, all grown up and everything!

Looking Back
Luke 9:51-62

Remember Lot's wife. While some would like to go back and live in the *"good old days,"* it is never the will of God to do so, nor is it where God wants you to be. Paul said, *"What things were gain to me, those I counted loss for Christ. Forgetting those things which are behind and reaching unto those things which are before."* Looking back on things too much with interest will bring a sudden halt to all that God has planned for those who must look ahead.

Jesus said, *"Follow me"*...period (Luke 9:23). He did not say you could follow Him and someone else at the same time. It is safe to say, what He said was to follow Him first. Follow Him where? At this occasion, He was going to Jerusalem, and at Jerusalem was the cross on which He was to die. This cross would open up a passageway for any person to come and find real life as God intended it to be.

Note the three would-be followers in this passage. One evidently was secure in the comforts of home. He might have been living the *"Life of Riley."* Jesus said to him, "If you want to follow me, you must consider sacrificing all that you have." Foxes have better sleeping places in holes than you might have by following Jesus. Jesus came not to live, but to die. Did this man follow Jesus? I hope so!

The next man Jesus asked to follow Him was sensible and caring for his family. He wanted first to bury his father. Jesus said in a sense, that burying the dead was important, but not as important as following Him. Someone else could do those things such as conducting a funeral. Did this man follow Christ? I hope so!

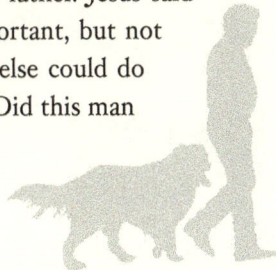

The third man said he would follow Jesus, but wanted to say farewell to his family. He was sensitive in calling on his loved ones and telling them about the will of God in his life. Jesus said, *"No man, having put his hands to the plough and looking back, is fit for the kingdom of God!"* Did he follow Him? I hope so!

Bigger barns usually take priority over the opportunity of suffering for Christ. Paul wanted to *know him, and the power of his resurrection, and the fellowship of his sufferings.* Looking back will always make the secondary primary in one's life. Following Christ first means understanding the difference between what is important and what is imperative. Telling others how to be born again is far more important than burying the dead. Looking back will silence the kingdom's work. And if we are not advancing the kingdom's work, we are not fit to go there! Looking back means we have left our first love. Following Christ means we are to be looking ahead.

— Connect

*Looking back will always cause lost opportunities
which will never happen the same again.*

JUST A THOUGHT...
*Looking back does not mean one will not go to heaven,
it just means one is not fit for heaven.*

"Lord, If You Had Been Here"

John 11:21

And some of them said, Could not this man, which opened the eyes of the blind, have caused that even this man should not have died (John 11:37)?

*There you go again...*questioning God! If God were God, He could have stopped the mighty earthquake from erupting in the South Seas of Asia which left the tsunami victims losing all they ever had in this world. God could have stopped more than 200,000 Indonesians from perishing in a flood which had biblical proportions. Pundits are speaking out against the character of an all-powerful, all-knowing, and ever-present God, saying, *"Carest thou not that we perish?"* Even using His divine name in doing so by saying, *"Lord, if you had been here, my brother had not died."* Where was God on 9/11 or on December 24, 2004?

In spite of this crowd, hearts and pocketbooks of more than 7 billion persons from all over the world have opened and are pouring out their prayers and financial support. Over 5 billion dollars came to the aid of hurting families having faced the greatest tsunami disaster they have ever seen, and rightfully so, I might add. Former Secretary Powell said, *"I have never seen anything like this."*

Where are the so-called experts when it comes to the more than 430,000 who die each year in America from the use of tobacco? Where are they who are calling an absolute halt to the murder of more than 1.5 million unborn babies each year in America by way of abortion? Why is it that Congress does not address the deaths of more than 17,000 each year from the use of alcohol? Rather than accepting

the blame for fatalities from our own tolerances, they blame God for some natural tragedy. What is wrong with these people?

The Bible says Jesus loved Martha, her sister Mary, and Lazarus. Jesus loves all people, yet Jesus did not come to heal or stop earthquakes, He came to save all people whom He loves from sin. He tasted death for every man. In addition to His saving blood, He sends sustaining grace to endure and to encounter the rain that falls on the just as well as on the unjust.

He listens to our cries. God heard the cry of His people in Egypt living under hard bondage as well as the cry from a crucified criminal, *"Lord, remember me when you come into your kingdom. Indeed, he is touched with the feelings of our infirmities."*

He is alive and will be forever interceding on our behalf at the right hand of God. He is the resurrection and the life. *It is appointed for all men once to die.* The hope facing the ultimate of any disaster is that there is a resurrection. He says, *"I am the resurrection and the life. Whosoever liveth and believeth in me shall never die. Believest thou this?"*

Where was God on December 24, 2004? He was with me, facing the worst ice storm I have ever seen and being without electricity for almost 7 days, as well as with the thousands of Indonesians whose hearts were broken, which remain scarred to the deepest degree. He is the great I AM of whom none would know what to do or where to go without him!

— *Connect* —

We must believe that God will be with us in life as well as in death. When it comes time to face death, in sickness or in misfortune, He will be at our side. Oh yes, He will!

JUST A THOUGHT...
God has promised in His Word that He would never leave us nor forsake us.

Our Father
Matthew 6:9

Any father who dangles his infant son over a high-rise balcony does not deserve to be a father! Any father who parties all night long and awakens the next morning finding his daughter has been kidnapped is totally irresponsible as a man and as a father. Any father who leaves his family just for the sake of becoming a National League Football Coach is no role model for any young athlete.

When I see these kinds of fathers, I ask, who was their father? Where is the old adage we were raised with: *"He is a chip off the old block,"* or, *"Like father, like son."* It is no wonder that we are living with a generation of kids cursing their fathers. Our children need a "daddy" (*Abba Father*) who literally *"hung the moon."*

And they can have such a Father. He is known in the Bible as the *Father of the Lord Jesus Christ* (II Cor. 1:3), as well as the Father to all who receive Him by faith, who become the sons of God (John 1:12).

Our Father is the heavenly Father. For Him to be Our Heavenly Father, one has to be born again, born from above. If you have been born from above, then you are my brother and my sister in the family of God. There are many earthly fathers, but only one heavenly Father.

Our Father is always at home. *"...which art in heaven...."* When the poor wayfaring traveler has taken his last steps in this world, Our Father will welcome His children home.

Our Father is always holy. *"Hallowed be thy name."* His name is not to be taken in vain—His name is Holy, there is no other name like it under heaven.

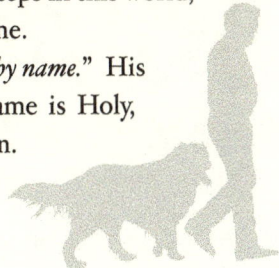

Our Father is always to be praised. We say, *"Hallelujah."* It is interesting that every known dialect pronounces the word *hallelujah* the same way. Let all the family of God rise, lifting up holy hands, praising Him from whom all blessings flow—He is worthy.

Our Father is always our help in a time of need. The supplier of our daily bread, the forgiver of our sins, and the deliverer from the paths of evil. His hands are not short that they can not save, nor His ears deaf that they can not hear. His heart is moved with compassion when He looks on the multitudes. He is our hope in a world headed for hell.

Our Father always desires to have more children. He loves all of His children. Children whose father is the devil can be adopted into Our Father's family. That which is born of the flesh can be born of the Spirit. If one is not born again, he can not see or enter the kingdom of Our Father. If any come to Him, He will cast none away.

—*Connect*—

*Call on Him, He is waiting and eager to listen
to what you have to say.*

JUST A THOUGHT...
Do you remember a time when Our Father was not your Father?

God's Marines
Matthew 5:9

"...for they shall be called the children of God."

The world has witnessed *mass destruction* of human life which has claimed the lives of tens of thousands in recent years. The wars in Kuwait, Iraq, Afghanistan, and Israel, and the rapid waves of multiple hurricanes in Florida and the massive tsunami sweeping away people in Indonesia have made it impossible for survivors in these places ever to be the same.

Where is God when disaster strikes, leaving heartaches and scars which seem to never heal? God is seen in His children, running with hearts of compassion, strong backs, deep pockets, and with helping hands. Under those hard hats, they come as Christians, doctors and nurses, contractors, businessmen, lawyers, politicians, school teachers, carpenters, preachers, policemen, firemen, electricians, and plumbers. These come ready to assure the victims that *"this too will soon pass,"* pain as they know it will subside, and peace will reign. They are *God's Marines* from various selective, civil, and private services storming the beaches of despair, bringing help and hope with them.

There is an affirmation of those who have heard the call, volunteered their lives and have been sworn in under oath devoting their services as trustworthy, honorable, and with true feelings of sympathy. They are the real troops which are the only threat to fear. Were it not for the will of God in their lives and for self-gratification, the often thankless response would render the *"let the world go to hell"* attitude. The rewards for the children of God are not earthly, but rather heavenly. God knows

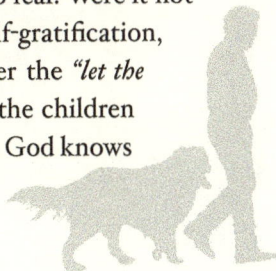

His peacemakers, and will affirm their work one day with those coveted words, "My beloved children, *well done!*"

There is a deep appreciation for God's servants. They have my adoration, my interest, and my endorsement. I will stand with humbleness in saluting these for going where most men fear to tread. Those who come with the truth of God's work and Word are the real peacemakers—I appreciate that!

There is an utmost admiration to those who give the ultimate sacrifice—their lives. Many have died in battle fighting for freedom, safety, and for others to have quiet and peaceful lives. I stand in awe regarding these! These have my prayers and thanks.

Jesus Christ, the Son of God, left the glories of heaven, came in the volume of the book written of Him, took on Himself the form of a servant, died on a cross for the sacrifice of sin, and rose on the third day. He shed His innocent blood for a guilty sinner like me, that I might know the peace and the pardoning of my sin. Today, I have peace because of the Son of God, Jesus Christ, my Savior!

— *Connect* —

He took my place, that I might one day be in His place which He has prepared for me.

JUST A THOUGHT...
The more peacemakers, the less troublemakers there will be.

A People for His Name
Acts 15:14

Ladies and Gentlemen: May I introduce

to you the new Mr. and Mrs. Donald Trump. And all the would-be brides-to-be drooled with desire as the commanding announcement came to seal the anticipated moment. On January 22, 2005, Melania Knauss became the new Mrs. Donald Trump, a new beginning for her with a new name. *The Donald* knows how to throw a wedding (his third!), a wedding that cost in the millions. Some say, "A marriage made in heaven!" Really?

On April 8, 2005, Prince Charles of England married Carmillia Parker Bowels. The entire world will be observing the royalty of...another wedding for both of them. Carmillia will take Charles's name, and one day be the wife of the King of England. A longtime dream come true... for Prince Charles and Carmillia!

The wedding of all weddings is yet to happen. It will make weddings like these appear to be rags compared to the riches which the Father will bestow upon the wedding of Christ and the church. It is called the *marriage of the Lamb*, the bride has made herself ready. *She is arrayed in fine linen, clean and white: for the fine linen is the righteousness of the saints. Come hither and I will show you the Lamb's wife.*

To become the bride of the groom, one must be prepared to take on his name. It speaks of a marital bond of intimacy and togetherness. *The two shall be one.* I'm kind of old-fashioned; I believe that the bride is to bear the name of her husband and that marriage should be between one man and one woman for a lifetime.

In the spiritual realm, there is no bond or free, Jew or Gentile, God is calling out *a people for his name*. He has planned a wedding for His Son; the Holy Spirit has been marshaled to seek the bride. Soon the Son will come in the air to take His bride, and so shall we forever be with Him in the mansion which He has prepared for us. He has chosen you to be part of that ceremony, bear His name, and take upon yourself His nature. That name which is above all names, which clarifies who God is and what we should be.

Believing and trusting in that name, the only name whereby men must be saved, at the moment of salvation the believer is enabled to be one in Him. Becoming one in Him, we seek to please and to honor Him. We promise to love and to cherish Him, in sickness or in health, for richer or for poorer, for better or for worse, and to cleave only unto Him and Him only as long as we shall live.

A people for His name will be carried unto the next generation as we win others for Christ. It is called the great commission: preaching, reaching, teaching, and baptizing in the name of Jesus. A people for His name will bring people into conformance of His Son for which we have been made. A people for His name will one day be called out of this world for a marriage made in heaven. A people for His name will celebrate the joy of forever being in His presence. A new you!

— Connect —

We give to Him all our worldly belongings,
and in doing so, we seal our vows..

JUST A THOUGHT...
    His name is far better than riches.

Perpetual Praise
Psalm 145

"*Thank you*" were words from Iraq's new interim prime minister, Ayad Allawi, addressing a joint congress in Washington. He promised America, as he patted himself on his breast with thanks for our sacrifices, that liberating his country of dictatorship and our efforts of freeing Iraq of terrorism have not been in vain. His praise will be a lasting one and equally so for some 25 million Iraqis.

These words struck a real chord in my heart as I referenced this address to our great and good God for freeing us from the holds of Satanism and bondage which grips lives with shackled chains of sin. The earmark of all believers is praise for God's work in redemption. Now and one day standing in His presence with *ten thousand times ten thousand and thousands of thousands* we will say in unison with a loud voice, "*Worthy is the Lamb which was slain to receive power, and riches, and wisdom, and strength, and honor, and glory, and blessings.*"

Great is the LORD, and greatly to be praised; and his greatness is unsearchable. (3) *My mouth shall speak the praise of the LORD: and let all flesh bless his holy name for ever and ever* (21).

I will speak (every day and for eternity) *of the glorious honor and his majesty and of his wondrous works* (5) because I am His child. And since He is my Father, and my everlasting Father, I will praise Him for ever and ever. God takes great pleasure and delight when His children humble themselves and lift up holy hands in praise unto Him and His name. "Thank you," and with praise now and forever.

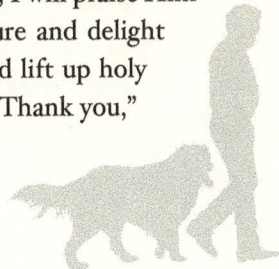

The LORD is good to all: and his tender mercies are over all his works (9). This is the character of God and because He is the same yesterday, today and forever. His praise will ring throughout *his everlasting kingdom, and his dominion throughout all generations. The LORD is righteous in all his ways, and holy in all his works.* "Thank you," dear God. *for making known to the sons of men of your mighty acts, and the glorious majesty of your kingdom.*

God's praise is perpetual because *he is full of compassion and great in mercy.* "Thank you," dear God, for lifting us from the miry clay, and the care which is above your care for the sparrows. Your ear hears our cries and prayers. "Thank you," for preserving us for thy everlasting kingdom.

We will sing of thy righteousness...(7) O for a thousand tongues to sing my great Redeemer's praise, the glories of my God and King, the triumphs of His grace. O Lord my God, when I in awesome wonder consider all the worlds Thy hands have made, I see the stars, I hear the rolling thunder, Thy pow'r throughout the universe displayed! Until that day, He will keep me till the river rolls its water at my feet. Then He will bear me safely over where my loved ones I shall meet. Yes, I will sing the wondrous story of the Christ who died for me. Sing it with the saints in glory, gathered by the crystal sea! Then I shall bow in humble adoration, and there proclaim, My God how great Thou art! And all the people said, *"Hallelujah, hallelujah!"*

Connect

Thank you, thank you, thank you for loving us as we are, and loving us so much as to not leave us the way we are.

JUST A THOUGHT...
One can not praise Him continually while complaining about one's problems.

And He Gave Some
Pastors and Teachers
Ephesians 4:11

A couple entered their pastor's office looking as though the weight of the world was resting on their shoulders. They said to him, "We are having a major problem that is dividing our home. We need help." After listening to their situation, he kindly said to them, "If you had been in church last Wednesday evening for Bible study, you would have learned how to cope with and handle this problem."

And he gave (to the church) *some...pastors and teachers.* The church is looked upon in the Scriptures as a flock of sheep. Sheep need constant care which comes only from a shepherd. A shepherd will lead sheep beside still waters, keep the sheep from the wolves, and will feed the sheep with the Word of God. A shepherd will teach sheep by example how to walk, work, and win in life. A shepherd (pastor) is God's gift, one to be revered, respected, and regarded as a man of God. How few sheep value this heavenly gift for the use of their spiritual development and their earthly deployment.

In the physical, sheep after their kind can never become a shepherd (herdsman). However, in the spiritual realm, God calls some from the sheepfold to become gifted pastors and teachers. A gift that is never rescinded—*gifts that are without repentance.* There is no retirement, no relinquishing, and no retreat in this calling. He is called to be always there, his phone always rings, and his door always swings. A

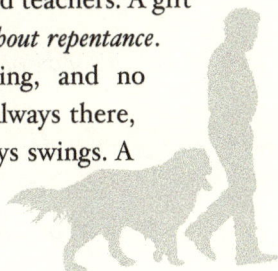

pastor whose voice is only known by the sheep of his fold. Sheep who fail to listen to their shepherd are prone to wander from the fold.

According to Eph. 4:11-13, these pastors and teachers are for the maturing of the saints for the work of the ministry, the building up of the body of Christ. This work is to be carried out till we all come into the fullness of the stature of Christ. Listen, he is trying to help you.

Shepherds not only prepare the sheep for service, but they pray for the sheep. Jesus, the Good Shepherd prayed for His sheep (see John 17). His prayer was that God would keep them while they are in this world. This world is made up of cults—beliefs which structure a culture. A culture which has a Bible foundation will never be led astray by any strange doctrine. The system of antichrist is part of this world and they take no pity. They are like ravening wolves, not sparing the flock. Much of the pastor's job is taken up by praying for the protection of his sheep. Thank him today for his prayers.

A pastor of a local church is somewhat like a parent to a home. Many within his congregation he has led to Christ in a new birth experience. He has been there in their spiritual infancy, worked with them through their spiritual adjustments, and taught them to grow into strong men and women for God. He may not preach the Bible as well as other preachers in town, but no other pastor has a better Bible to preach from than the one he carries to the pulpit every Sunday. He loves his people, no matter what. No matter what? No matter what! Some sheep are those which only a...pastor can love.

And he gave some...pastors and teachers. As in every classroom there must be a teacher, and in every courtroom there needs to a judge, so in every church, there needs to be a pastor and teacher. Thank you, God, for this lifelong gift to us!

— *Connect* —

Go ahead and make his day, thank him for being your pastor.

JUST A THOUGHT...
*And while you are thanking him,
thank the Chief Shepherd for sending His pastor your way.*

The Philippian Jailor

Acts 16:25-34

This is not a time for crybabies; it's time for real men of faith to stand up, forgetting what is present and tend to the Father's business—the time is urgent and of necessity. It will either be suicide or salvation, heaven or hell, death or life for the jailor at Philippi. Enter Paul and Silas who throw out the lifeline to a sinking ship. This is one of the great stories of the Bible of winning the lost in the nick of time. Some may call this deathbed salvation. If so, it is as good as any!

Singing in jail! Paul and Silas had cast a demon from a lady. This was a good thing, but for that they were severely beaten and thrown in prison. Their backs were against the wall and their feet were secured in shackles and chains. Licking their wounds was not the setting for these two missionaries. Their darkest hour for some would be their worst nightmare. For these, it was church time. They were heard praying and singing praises unto God in a jail cell. They sang at the top of their voices where everyone heard them. I like this!

When you find yourselves between a rock and a hard place, where seemingly decisions are being made for you, and it's pitch black, pray like mad and sing! Songs in the night can somehow get you through to the break of the day. You are there for a reason, so prepare yourselves and tend to God's business.

Sleeping on the job. This warden did not have the foggiest idea what would happen on third trick that night. He had done his job; he beat these *sidewinders* to a pulp and fastened them to a wall. He protected

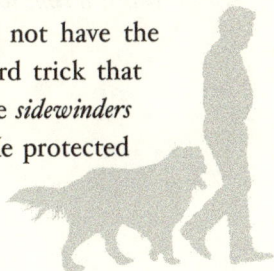

his job by securing these religious zealots. Turn out the lights and take a nap.

A miracle right before his sleepy eyes. An earthquake shook the prison doors open and the iron bands fell right off all the prisoners. He thought, no one will believe this in a million years, so he drew his sword and was about to fall on it when he heard a loud voice... *"Do thyself no harm, for we are all here."*

Salvation that is joyful. This jailor which has been shocked into reality, asked the most important question any man can ask anywhere, anytime. The jailor responded immediately and sensibly by saying, *"Sirs, what must I do to be saved?" They said, "Believe on the Lord Jesus Christ and you will be saved and your house."* Then a discipleship class took place, as Paul and Silas spoke unto them the Word of God.

The jailor washed and bound up the wounds which he had made on these men of God, and followed the Lord in believer's baptism along with members of his family who also believed in God, rejoicing in this so great salvation.

What difference a decision for Christ can make in your life and the life of your family. How sensitive Paul and Silas were to the urgency of the hour in leading the jailor to Christ. And what a lesson for all of us to apply our lives as soul-winners for Christ. One never knows when it may be the last time for someone to be saved.

— *Connect* —

The peace of God will enable any to enjoy the most tested times.

JUST A THOUGHT...
   It is still time to get in, even on your deathbed!

How to Pray for a Nation

Nehemiah 1

We pray for our children to get well when they are sick, we pray for safety as we drive from place to place, and we pray for our needs to be met. But how does one pray for a nation like America where 300 million people live every day? America is under attacks of terrorism, and we are being warned of its pending consequences every day. People are praying for safety, freedom, and trust. All we have known for better than 225 years is now in jeopardy!

Nehemiah prayed for a nation, Daniel prayed for a nation, David prayed for a nation, and Jesus prayed for a nation and a world! The Bible tells us to pray so all may lead a quiet and peaceable life. Like Esther, *"We have come to the kingdom for such a time as this"*...to pray for our nation!

When you pray, specifically include the President of the United States, the most powerful man in the free world. He is our leader and he is walking point in ridding America and the world of terrorism. They covet our prayers today! On his behalf, ask for divine wisdom and strength for him and his staff.

Praying for a nation means praying according to the needs of a nation (Neh. 1:3). Nehemiah prayed for the rebuilding of the walls which were the "safety net" of his nation. Pray today for protection in America from the forces of evil men in the world. *"In God we trust,"* is America's only hope and protection.

Praying for a nation means getting serious in praying and fasting (Neh 1:4). Nehemiah *wept, mourned, and*

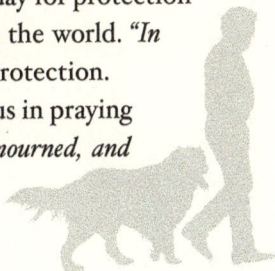

fasted as he prayed for certain days. Daniel prayed and fasted for a nation for 21 days. Jesus fasted and prayed for Jerusalem. At times, Jesus would pray all night. Compare this kind and time of praying to our kind and time of praying!

Praying for a nation means confessing the sins of a nation (Neh. 1:6-9). Israel had sinned, became disobedient, and was a rebellious people. Today begin confessing the sins of murdering unborn babies, divorcing of God from our schools, immorality, drugs, sexual promiscuity, and anti-Semitism.

Praying for a nation means one who prays believes that God can answer any prayer (Neh 1:11). Nehemiah prayed and asked God *to be attentive to his prayer.* David prayed, *"Hear my prayer, O God, and attend unto my prayer."* Anyone who can pray for a nation, must believe that only God can answer such a prayer. *He that comes to God must believe that he is a rewarder of them that diligently seek him.*

— *Connect* —

Pray now to the God in heaven. He will hear our cry;
He will forgive and heal our land.

JUST A THOUGHT...
Ask yourself this question: If my country would
depend on my prayers, how safe would it be?

Questions at the Cross of Jesus
John 19:25

Now there stood at the cross of Jesus...
John 19:25.

I was tense, exhausted, drained, and moved to tears as I watched Mel Gibson's film, *The Passion of the Christ*. From the garden to Golgotha, I felt like I was part of the crowd that followed Jesus during the last twelve hours of His life. Every muscle and nerve in my body flinched as I watched Him being scourged. I followed Him down through the Via Della Rosa as it brought us to the foot of a hill that looked like a skull. I climbed that hill and found myself standing where others were standing, at the foot of the cross looking into an abandoned piece of humanity, totally forsaken by God and helpless from the hands of caring loved ones.

Questions saturated the scene for more than two hours in that film. Questions like when Jesus asked the mob, "*Whom seek ye?*" The questions directed to Peter: "*Are you not his disciple?*" A present-day question from Pilate: "*What is truth?*" But the most notorious question came from Christ on the cross: "*My God, my God why have you forsaken me?*"

Hanging with criminals on a cross, what kind of a life is this? Jesus said, "*This is eternal life that you might know the only true God and Jesus Christ whom he has sent.*" Only in Christ are we alive unto God; outside of Him we are dead in trespasses and sin. Life in Christ can tolerate crumbs from a rich man's table or the dogs licking at one's sores. Yet so poor, in Him, I am so rich.

Everyone today is waiting to hear the truth. Truth does not rest totally with science, religion, or

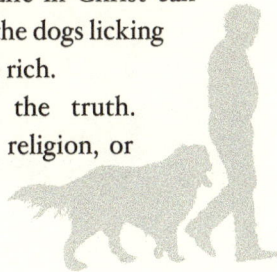

philosophy, but lies in a person. Jesus is that person where the fullness of the Godhead dwells. He is the truth, the personification of God in the flesh, and without error.

As you face His cross you might ask, "Why did Jesus come and die by way of the crucifixion?" It was as if God was saying the capitol punishment is worthy of the crime. Yet in the midst of the brutality, the gore and blood, stands a man. Only a God-man could have withstood such sufferings and such a cruel death.

He said, "*Father, forgive them, for they know not what they do.*" What does Jesus want? He wants you and me along with the repentant thief to be with Him in paradise. A million times more than Uncle Sam, Jesus loves you and wants you!

The question which is asked about *the Passion* is this: *Who killed Jesus?* The Jews, the Romans, who is to be blamed? Ironic as it is in the film, we are told it was the actual hand of Mel Gibson holding the nail as the hammer dropped, plunging it into the hand of Jesus. Mr. Gibson said, "*It was my sin that caused Him to die.*" Indeed it was Mr. Gibson's sin and my sin and your sin, and the sin of the world which caused Him to die.

— *Connect*

Here is a question for you. What will you do with Jesus?

JUST A THOUGHT...
Behold the man!

The Real Family Man
Psalm 128

*President George W. Bush's statements on
families/marriage:*

"A great deal is at stake in this matter," Bush said. "For ages, in every culture,
human beings have understood that traditional marriage is critical to the well-
being of families... And changing the definition of traditional marriage will
undermine the family structure."

A few renowned families in the news:

Three members of a family were found dead on Sam Donaldson's
ranch in New Mexico. The teenage son, Delbert Posey, of that family
is being charged for their murders. Sam Donaldson said, *"This was the
all-American family."* Eric Douglas, youngest son of Oscar-winning actor,
Kirk Douglas, was found dead of an overdose of drugs.

Dysfunctional families of recent days:

Michael Jackson was charged as a pedophile child molester. Kobe
Bryant's case as a sex offender. Scott Peterson serving a life sentence
for the double murder of his wife, Lacy, and their unborn son, Connor.
President Bill Clinton will always be remembered of his encounter with
Monica Lewinski.

Will the real family man please stand up!
Blessed is every one that feareth the LORD; that walketh
in his ways. For thou shalt eat the labor of thine hands: happy
shalt thou be, and it shall be well with thee. Thy wife shall

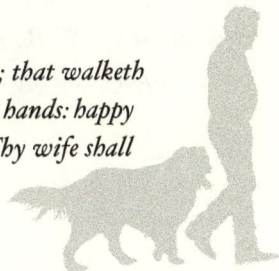

be as a fruitful vine by the sides of thine house: thy children like olive plants round about thy table. Behold, that thus shall the man be blessed that feareth the LORD. The LORD shall bless thee out of Zion: and thou shalt see the good of Jerusalem all the days of thy life. Yea, thou shalt see thy children's children, and peace upon Israel (Psalm 128.)

The real family man is not defined by the ACLU, NOW, or Planned Parenthood, but rather from the Bible. He is a committed man to the Lord. One who reveres the Lord in his worship, his walk with his Lord, and his work ethic. The Lord's ways are different from the ways of the world—that is a given. If the family structure is to keep the moral foundation stable in this day, we need real family men who follow biblical principles, men who are staunch, steadfast, and dyed-in-the-wool men of God.

The real family man has a wife, one wife. The angels asked Abraham, *"Where is thy wife?"* The real family man has a wife who is loving, supportive, and likewise as with her husband, submissive. *Submitting yourselves one to another in the fear of God.* She is ever true to her calling as a wife. Also, a real family man is defined by having his children who are on his team like planted, fixed flower pots gracing the home. And even to the fourth and fifth generation with his children's children. The real family man is a man whose love of his life is the local church. *And thou shalt see the good of Jerusalem all the days of thy life.*

—Connect—

*You and I will leave some kind of a legacy.
What will history record about our families?*

JUST A THOUGHT...
President George W. Bush is right on the family, the Bible is right on the family, and the real family man is right on the family.

Reading to Get Rich

Colossians 3:16

How many copies of the Word of God are found in your home today? Two, five, eight maybe? How much of it dwells in your heart? Little compared to what should be there, I bet. We have no trouble in finding a Bible somewhere when we need to, but it is very difficult in finding a verse in a Bible when we need help in complicated situations which develop in our lives.

The successful Christian today is one who is rich in the Word of God. One who is able to draw the water of life from its deep wells at any given moment of time. The best of some is that they remember something the preacher said sometime ago, but can't remember exactly what it was or where it is found in the Bible. Maybe it is because there is too much dust on their Bibles. The Bible is carried more today in hand to church once a week than carried in the heart daily.

The Bible says *the Word of God was made flesh and dwelt among us* (John 1:14), referring to Christ, the logos, the living Word of God. To some degree, that happens to the believer when the Word dwells richly in the heart. These become living epistles known and read of men.

I have been taught and trained to read the Word of God through each year. By reading three chapters each day and five on Sunday, all 66 books of the Bible can be read in one year. The Bible says, *"Blessed is he that readeth it..."* Question: How long have you been saved and how many times have you read the Word of God completely through? You probably

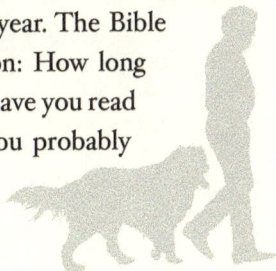

knew I would ask that question, didn't you? Regarding the Bible, if you have never read it through, then why don't you make a commitment right before God to read it through this year. If you can not do it in a year, take two years or three to do it, but "just do it!" Do not be overwhelmed by its volume; it is a lifetime book for a lifetime task.

The Word of God is likened to a seed. When planted it brings forth fruit, and fruit in abundance. Some that fell on good ground brought forth some 30, some 60 fold.

What has it done for me for more than 50 years as a child of God? It has settled the question of salvation forever. *Faith comes by hearing and hearing by the word of God.* I was *born again not by a corruptible seed, but of incorruptible seed, by the word of God, which liveth and abideth forever.* It has been bearing fruit in my life since conception. It enables me to know sin and how to deal with sin. *Thy word have I hid in my heart that I might not sin against thee. If we confess our sins, he is faithful and just to forgive us our sins and cleanse us from all unrighteousness.* If the Word of God dwells in us richly, we can overcome Satan and his temptations. Anyone who has never been tempted by the devil, stand up. The mighty Christ Himself overcame all that Satan could throw at Him from hell for 40 days. Satan was defeated by the wielding power of the Word of God. So, just how rich are you? And do you know what Jude chapter 2 says?

— *Connect* —

Every word of God is pure, but you must read every word to feel it.

J U S T   A   T H O U G H T ...
        Jude chapter 2! I thought so!

Remember Lot's Wife
Genesis 19:26

But his wife looked back from behind him, and she became a pillar of salt. There is only one thing we remember about Lot's wife given to us from Scripture, and that is she became *a pillar of salt!* We do not know her name, where she came from, or anything about her family. We do know she was married to Lot, Abraham's nephew. She and Lot had two daughters and the family was living in Sodom when God rained fire down from heaven in judgment to overthrow the wicked cities of Sodom and Gomorrah.

The story is found in Genesis 19—Lot (*a righteous man*) and his entire family are found living quietly and comfortably in a land populated by a wicked and adulterous people. The Bible says, *"Lot was vexed (troubled) with the filthy conversation of the wicked"* (2 Pet. 2:8). Lot was troubled living in this land of sin, but chose to do nothing about it. He got himself and those he loved into a real mess. His sons-in-law mocked him, his wife turned into salt, and he commited incest with his daughters. Were it not for Peter's comments about this matter, we all could safely conclude that the entire family was steeped in sin and lost. But—*God knows how to deliver the godly out of temptation and reserve the unjust unto the day of judgment to be punished.*

Remember Lot's wife because she looked back and became a pillar of salt (Gen. 19:26). As they were fleeing, Mrs. Lot lagged behind and looked back intently with longing and desire. She got out of Sodom, but Sodom never got out of her. The loss of a quickening and sensitive spirit of the things of the Lord is that of a backslidden and carnal

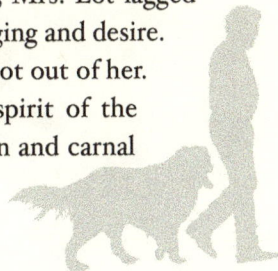

state. Was Mrs. Lot saved? Whether she was or not is not the issue. *God is no respecter of persons; it rains on the just as well as on the unjust.* If we fail to adhere and obey His commands—His judgment rest at our feet. *Remember Lot's wife!*

Remember Lot's wife because she lost her life while trying to save it. She was happy there and became unhappy having to leave that God-forsaken land. Sodom is not where one would want to raise a family. No one can merit one degree of God's favor by living with a carnal interest in a sinful environment. *"Make no provision for the flesh."* There is not a *"dime's worth"* of gain that can be found anywhere in this world. *Remember Lot's wife!*

Remember Lot's wife because she left nothing worthwhile for anyone to follow. What a legacy to leave! What will those who will one day read of your life's story have to talk about? Will they have *"precious memories"* to remember? Things which will be permanently etched in the minds of one who abstained from the very appearance of evil, having not one thing said about them which brings a reproach upon the name of God? *Keep thyself pure; give no place to the devil. Remember Lot's wife!*

— Connect —

What's in your legacy?

JUST A THOUGHT...
See that you have all your family on your team.

Rendering to Caesar and Rendering to God
Matthew 22:21

"I can't believe what I am seeing!" If what we as a nation and world are witnessing, would have been told us only 10 to 15 years ago, many would have said, *"I don't believe what I am hearing."* The world has taken the things which are God's and made them Caesar's. And the church has sat back and let them do it without a fight. All of a sudden we have woke up and those things which we have held so dear for so long are now under Caesar's control.

Caesar has taken over the authority of telling us what is moral and what is not. It is no longer wrong to look upon men with men and women with women as something which is immoral. Today, homosexuality is politically correct in the minds of this present generation and being accepted as a norm in every sector of society. It was God's *"talking points"* for all the preachers, teachers, and lawyers to make clear the sin of homosexuality. The liberal press now defines to us what is okay, and gender is whatever one wants it to be. The homosexuals have taken over in politics, classrooms, TV programs, books, newspapers, and even our pulpits in our churches. It's time for the church to take back what they have rendered to Caesar!

Caesar has defined for us what is life and what is a mass of tissue. They are now telling us it is okay for a woman to choose to abort this mass inside the womb.

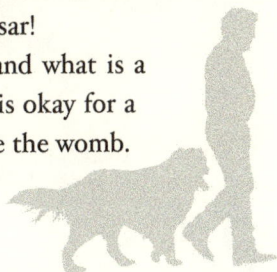

They have doctored it up by saying, *"a woman's right to choose."* To choose what, I ask? Choose to kill the baby living in her "tummy"? Does she have the right to kill the baby living in her nursery? Because of abortion, we are giving our tax money to fund places like Planned Parenthood to counsel and to advise the mother what she wants to do. Their word is to calm the mother-to-be, get her adjusted, and to help her through this traumatic event which will take place. Why, I ask; what is the big deal if it is only the removal of a mass of blood and tissue? The truth of it all is that the church has let Caesar be God to redefine what was once written about life and death.

Have we not learned by now what it has meant to this country when Caesar removed God from our classrooms by not permitting our kids to pray? Kids now are taking guns to school and killing their buddies. ACT scores are at an all-time low. Teenage suicide is at an all-time high. Drugs are used and alcohol flows in the hallways like water from a drinking fountain. Teenage pregnancy is heard of more than when it was a "hush-hush" commentary. This is what happens when Caesar gets ahold of what belongs to God. We have a generation which no longer knows how to blush!

— *Connect* —

Give Satan an inch and he will become your ruler.

JUST A THOUGHT...
God will bless anything we give back to Him.

The Sin of Lying
Genesis 3

"Liar, liar, pants on fire!" I remember telling my first lie. Boy, was it a humdinger! I stole a quarter from the bath towel shelf when I was about ten years old. The shelves were over the top of a little four-legged heater in the bathroom. The quarter was burning a hole in my pocket, so I bought a big oatmeal cake. In those days, they were as big as a saucer plate. It cost five cents and Mrs. Dufore gave me back four nickels. Mom always checked pockets before washing, so I had to do something with those four nickels. So I placed a nickel under each of those four legs of the little heater in the bathroom to hide them for more oatmeal cakes later.

Mom asked me if I had seen that quarter on the shelf in the bathroom (quarters were a lot of money in those days). I said, "No, Mamm." (Lie # one.) Mom not only did the washing, she did the cleaning too. Guess what? She found those four nickels, each of them under that four-legged bathroom heater. She asked me another question. "Clifford, do you know how those four nickels got under those four legs of the bathroom heater?" I thought this one through as to how I would answer her. I said, "Well, I guess that quarter fell from the shelf and *"busted"* up into four nickels!" (Lie # two.)

Mom not only did the washing and the cleaning, but she also could tell a lie when she heard one, and that was a big one! The price of those two lies was more than 25 cents. I have never been able to live that one down.

No one had to teach me to lie, it just came natural. I have never known a person of accountability who has

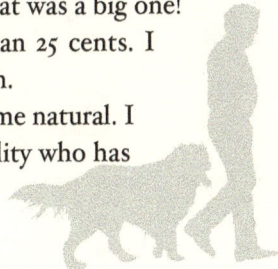

not told a lie (except God—who can not lie, Tit. 1:2). I have learned that telling a lie is an empty, worthless, shameful feeling. And most of the time, one has to tell a second lie to try to cover up the first one.

The first liar was Satan, when he said, God didn't really mean that Adam and Eve would die if they ate of the *tree of knowledge of good and evil* (Gen. 2:9; 3:4). Satan is a liar and the father of lies (John 8:44). We learn to tell lies because we were children of the devil before being saved. Guess what? Adam told a lie, Eve told a lie, Cain told a lie, and so on. Believing Satan's lies is a downward road to hell.

When lies are told, we want to hide, or hide something (Gen. 3:8), then we become afraid (Gen. 3:10), and we try to cover it up by blaming someone else (Gen. 3:12). The guilt of telling a lie can be seen as quickly as you enter a room. You just can't cover it up!

—Connect—

If one can choose to tell a lie, one can choose to tell the truth.
Choose God to be your Father;
He will teach you the truth and how to tell the truth!

JUST A THOUGHT...
When telling the truth, you never have to
remember what you have said.

Those Who Stand
in the House of God
Psalm 135

The joy that is unspeakable and full of glory in serving Christ should be experienced in life as long as one can remember. One of my most favorite character studies in all the Bible is that of one named Anna (Luke 2). A widow who was 84 years old which departed not from the temple. She was found standing in church serving God with fastings and prayers.

Everything in the sea is not fish, but any fish that are alive today are in the sea. Likewise, not everybody found in the church today is part of the body of Christ. But, all believers that love the Lord are found standing somewhere in church. The Bible tells us not to forsake the assembling of ourselves together, but so much the more as we see the day approaching. Those found standing in the house of God are busy for the Lord, serving Him with their time, money, and talents, and enjoying every moment of it.

Praise ye the LORD. Praise ye the name of the LORD; praise him, O ye servants of the LORD. Ye that stand in the house of the LORD, in the courts of the house of our God, Praise the LORD; for the LORD is good: sing praises unto his name; for it is pleasant.

The difference between standing in church and standing outside of church is that of our "gods." Those not standing in the house of the LORD are found serving "gods" that they have made—gods that can not speak, can not see, can not hear, and are not alive. The gods

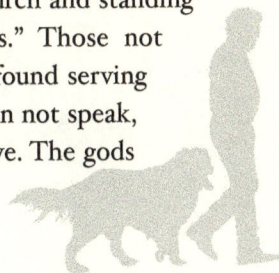

of gold and silver are the work of men's hands, which are like unto them that made them (15-18).

Our Lord is above all gods (5). He is good (3), He is great (5), He is glorious (9), and He is giving (12). We who are standing in church have got something to sing about and something to say about our God who is so pleasant and powerful.

It comes with the territory. That is, when God calls one to serve, there comes with that calling an obligation. An obligation to tell the truth about God and His plan. When we make a choice to follow Him, there comes with that choice an opportunity. An opportunity to share the great stories about God found in the Bible.

God chose Jacob and Israel to be his peculiar treasure (4). Through this nation would come the Messiah. One who would bring hope to the entire world. One who overcame all obstacles and opposition by following the Word of God. He called 12 disciples and with these followers, He turned the world upside down. After some three years of ministry, He suffered on a cross and died and was buried in a tomb for three days. However, He got up from that damning grave with a shout of victory. With this message in hand we become a voice in the wilderness, preparing those who will hear to get ready to meet the LORD, the greatest story ever told.

Those standing in church have got great stories to tell about our God. Stories of the *tokens and wonders* (9) which He has sent to tell of His power that human intelligence can not explain. From the crossing of the Red Sea, to the manna in the wilderness, to the tumbling of the walls of Jericho, enough stories which all the shelves in the entire world could not contain the volumes which could be written of them.

— Connect —

Cat got your tongue?

JUST A THOUGHT...
The greatest stories are Bible stories.

The Strength of One
Psa 133

Behold, how good and how pleasant it is for brethren to dwell together in unity! It is like the precious ointment upon the head, that ran down upon the beard, even Aaron's beard: that went down to the skirts of his garments; As the dew of Hermon, and as the dew that descended upon the mountains of Zion: for there the LORD commanded the blessing, even life for evermore.

"*I am proud that after September 11th all our people rallied to President Bush's call for unity to meet the danger. There were no Democrats. There were no Republicans. There were only Americans. How we wish it had stayed that way.*" John Kerry, July 29, 2004.

We have many unions today, but little unity. Families, marriages, businesses, politicians, churches, the Supreme Court, and even our beloved America are divided right down the middle. *"A house divided against itself shall not stand."*

While divisions at times are not all bad, and the formation of another can clarify, simplify, and even multiply, yet the strength of one can never be quantified.

Unity is found in God and comes from God. *The Lord your God is one Lord. Holy Father, keep through thine own name those whom thou hast given me, that they may be one.* When real unity is found, it is the stamp of God's image. When it comes from above, it like gravity flows downward till every fiber is affected and saturated. It begins at the head and will not consummate till everything in its path has been consecrated, changed, and brought into conformity with God's plan. When

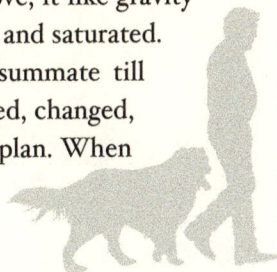

so, from the top to the foothills of the mountains, God's blessings are found.

The strength of one originates with the Father, one Father, our Father, the omnipotent God. *"My Father can do anything!"* He is not the Father of everyone, only the Father of the *brethren.* Anyone can become a son of our Father by way of the blood of Christ and a second birth into His family. *"You must be born again."* Unity in family gatherings are always *good and pleasant.* Those who still remain in the devil's family are divided, disgruntled, and one day will be destroyed.

The strength of one is when all in the family are found on the same page. When we dwell together in one accord, nothing can stop us. Even the gates of hell can not prevail against us. When disaster hits, we are one in body, soul, and spirit. Michael Jordan said, *"Talent wins games, teamwork wins championships."*

United brethren are those who are one in the blood, the book, and the blessed hope. One in the Savior, Jesus Christ who gave His life that all might be saved. Unified in preaching the everlasting Gospel of Christ to the world. The strength of one can reach this entire world in one generation.

— Connect —

I can do all things through Christ which strengthens me.

JUST A THOUGHT…
> *God and me...makes a majority.*

Strike Up the Band

Psalm 150

There was dancing in the streets as the largest turnout of voters ever went to the polls and cast their votes to give President George W. Bush a mandate and a second term for the next four years. He said in his acceptance speech, *"America has spoken,"* and did they ever. More votes were cast for this President than any other president before him. This election was historic as the people came out of church into the courts and cast their votes on issues of morality more than monetary values and social reform. Some 59 million *"undecided voters"* showed up and said, "This is the right time, the right man, and the right direction for our country." *Strike up the band!*

Praise him with the sound of the trumpet: praise him with the psaltery and harp. Praise him with the timbrel and dance: praise him with stringed instruments and organs. Praise him upon the loud cymbals: praise him upon the high sounding cymbals.

Praise the Lord! Let everything that has breath praise the Lord. When time changes into eternity, I believe there will be more of *us* than there will be of *them* as we praise our Lord for His greatness, His goodness, and for His glory. He will win and He will have the blessing of the people and the celebration will begin a new time and a new day without end. This is His day. *Strike up the band!*

Creatures (those who have breath) are to do what they were created to do. In this they complement their Creator. Creatures who have a soul are to do what they have been created to do and that is to worship

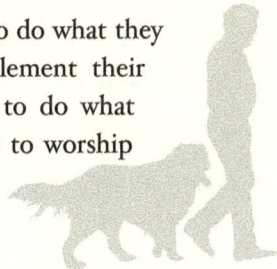

and ascribe their honor to their Creator God. This is praising God in His sanctuary, praising God in His dwelling place, and praising God throughout the universe for ever and ever. We have seen His power, felt His presence, and are secured with His program. Let the celebration begin and *strike up the band*.

The ceremony will be filled with instruments to do what they were made to do. These instruments will bring to life the words with sounds of perfection. Every note will be perfected, the pitch will be pleasant, and every player will be present to perform. Everything is in place; *strike up the band*.

The continuation of this jubilee will be without end. The people will be free from sin, sorrow, sickness, separation, and Satan. The former things are passed away and a new day has begun. The emancipation has been declared, the trumpet has sounded, and God's design for His family has finally arrived. We have come to the top of the mountain, the doxology is ready, and the finale sets a stage of permanence. There are no dead here (they are all in the lake of fire), all are alive and spiritually dead for eternity. Praise, worship, and singing will be the landscape of heaven as everything with breath will come together in unity in His praise.

— Connect —

Hallelujah, the church has spoken, strike up the band!

JUST A THOUGHT...
Where will you be found when the band prepares to sound?

A One-Word Summary
of a Christian
Psalm 130

The *"Hatchet Man"*—some of you will have to go back some 30 years to remember this man. His name is Charles W. "Chuck" Colson, the former top aide for one of the most brilliant minds of any president, President Richard Nixon. The world will hold him to the Watergate scandal and his prison term, but heaven will hold him to his conversion and a worldwide prison ministry.

He rose to the top and fell to the bottom in the political world. He became a born-again Christian and wrote a book about it, *Born Again*. Today, after almost 30 years since his conversion, his ministry is now in 60 countries, 50,000 workers, and ministers to over 250,000 prison inmates. He said, *"One of the lowest points in my life ended up being the greatest lesson I ever learned."*

Out of the depths have I cried unto thee, O LORD. Lord, hear my voice: let thine ears be attentive to the voice of my supplications. If thou, LORD, shouldest mark iniquities, O Lord, who shall stand? But there is forgiveness with thee, that thou mayest be feared (Psalms 130:1-4).

C.M. Ward once said: *"Sin will take you where you did not intend to go and keep you there longer than you intended to stay."* Let me add to this great statement, and that is, sin will not make anyone fit to come home. That is, unless the irreversible decline on a slippery slope takes an upward turn. The path of sin is a gradual regression

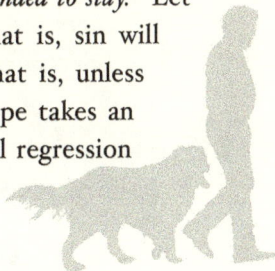

that has no bottom. One can bottom out in finances, in poverty, or even in depression. However, the step into sin is always downward, a step which will always have another one and one which will take you deeper into a deteriorated life. *"The heart is desperately wicked, who can know it."* There is no sin that can be imagined which can not be committed. That is the bad news. The good news is that there is no sin which can not be forgiven. Jesus died for all sin. There you have it, the one-word summary of a Christian: *forgiveness.*

He cried from the depths (of sin) and the Lord heard him. Jonah cried from the bottom of the whale's belly, the bottom of the mountains, the bottom of hell, and the Lord heard him. God is not hard of hearing, and no matter how far away from Him you are, He can hear the faintest cry instantly. All have sinned. There is none good, no not one, and no one can stand before God unless forgiveness has taken place. If God should mark our sins, who could stand and declare, "Not guilty"? There has been no one in the past, no one now, and not ever. We are all flawed, scarred, and marked vagabonds in this sinful world. The heart is indeed stained.

But there is forgiveness with God. He is plenteous in mercy and can redeem any man anytime of all of his iniquities. His nature is just that, a forgiving and compassionate heavenly Father. The degree of His forgiveness is compatible to the depths of sin and more so. There is no heinous sin that God can not forgive, and He is always standing at the gate to welcome any man home. The blood of His Son, Jesus Christ, is the only remedy for sin. Be it from a prison cell or a pew in a church, cry out to God now. Reverence to God can be your lifestyle as a forgiven Christian. He is listening, so call on Him now.

— Connect —

No man was made to bear the load of sin;
cast it on the Lord; He cares for you.

JUST A THOUGHT...
We can not be perfect, but we can be forgiven.

The Thanksgiving Equation

I Timothy 4:3,4

I read recently where a man was paid $200.00 during a sporting event to eat live worms! I tell you God's truth; God has never, ever led me to eat worms! However, if this man can ask God's blessing on those night crawlers before they squirm and slither their way into another black hole—then God bless him. I remember the first time eating boiled oysters right out of the shell. When I first saw those slimy creatures of God, praying at that moment was natural for me. I did not want to harm what God had made, so when they slid out of that shell, I did not create any obstruction as they slid to the bottomless pit.

During Thanksgiving week many will become gluttons as they abuse the body that God gave them in going for those *third and fourth helpings* from the table of blessings. There's nothing wrong with credit cards, but many will abuse them the day after Thanksgiving as they hit the shopping malls. This is a time when some will party and become engaged in sexual illicit encounters, lose their testimony, and break their marriage vows that they made to God and their spouse.

For every creature of God is good, and nothing to be refused, if it be received with thanksgiving: For it is sanctified by the word of God and prayer. If thou put the brethren in remembrance of these things, thou shalt be a good minister of Jesus Christ, nourished up in the words of faith and of good doctrine, whereunto thou hast attained.

Pastors need to remind their people that the *thanksgiving equation* is receiving the riches of all God's blessings with grace of the good things which He has

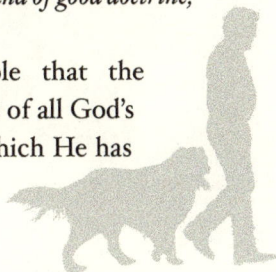

given to us. Things which are for our good and for His glory. It's harvest time, the reaping is in abundance. It is a time of blessings.

The greatest story in all the Bible of thanksgiving and using what God has given is that of the apostle Paul. He was in the way of utterly destroying God's people. Being in that way, his life turned as he turned in repentance falling on the road to Damascus. A question that changed his life which he will never forget is: *"Saul, Saul, why persecutest thou me?"* He allowed Jesus to enter his life and became the recipient of all that God can give any one man.

Compare Paul with Judas Iscariot. Rather than accepting what God had given him as a disciple of Christ, he allowed Satan to enter him which brought him to his demise. This man, who was one of the twelve, the one who betrayed Christ, is the greatest story in the Bible of ingratitude, ungratefulness, and unthankfulness. A question which will haunt Judas for eternity will be this: "Are you the man who betrayed the Master with a kiss?" For thirty pieces of silver, he sold his Lord and soul forever for a mess of pottage. The *thanksgiving equation* is when you receive and ask His blessings on all that He has given you.

— *Connect* —
Make sure the thanksgiving equation with the equal sign is always between God and you.

JUST A THOUGHT...
Thanksgiving is a time to remember.

"What Must I Do To Be Saved"

Acts 16:25-34

This is a classic question and one every inquirer must ask when confronted with salvation. This is the one question that must have the absolute correct answer before leaving this world. In this case, it came from one who was ready to die, either by the Roman sword or his own. Salvation is important at any time, but ever so important on one's deathbed. Paul wasted no time or words in telling this jailor what he had to do.

We as "the religious crowd" have done much to muddy the waters with this answer. Neither time nor space permits me to address all the answers which I have heard concerning this question. But what *"saith the Lord"* to this question? What does the Bible say is necessary for anyone to do about being saved, being born again, or becoming a child of the heavenly Father? Whatever the answer may be, that is what every person must do. If the Bible said we had to stand on our head and stack little green apples—that is exactly what we must do to become born again. Thank God the Scriptures don't say that!

The Bible tells us we must be saved/born again to go to heaven. *Jesus answered and said unto him, Verily, verily, I say unto thee, Except a man be born again, he cannot see the kingdom of God.* No person can go to heaven without being born again.

The Bible tells us why we need to be saved to go to heaven. *For all have sinned, and come short of the glory of God.* Also, *There is none righteous.* Again, *All we like sheep have gone astray.* The Bible says, *The wages of sin is death.* We are all sinners and if sinners got what they deserved, all sinners would go to hell.

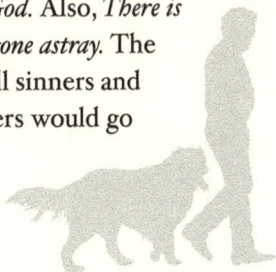

The Bible tells us when we need to be saved. *For he saith, I have heard thee in a time accepted, and in the day of salvation have I succoured* (helped) *thee: behold, now is the accepted time; behold, now is the day of salvation.* The only guaranteed time of salvation is NOW. (This does not mean the National Organization of Women!) No man can say what the next breath may bring.

The Bible tells us how to be saved. *For whosoever shall call upon the name of the Lord shall be saved.* If any would confess with their mouth and believe in their heart, that God has raised His Son from the dead, you will be saved. The word confess is a word which means to say it the same way or to say the same thing. God is asking us to believe in our heart and say with our mouths what He has already said about you and me. Pray and say something like this: *Lord, I believe in my heart that you sent your Son, Jesus Christ, to suffer and to die on the cross for me. I believe He arose from the dead on the third day. Right now, just as I am, I confess that I have sinned against you. In Jesus' name. Amen.*

The Bible tells us when one is saved, they can know they are saved. *These things have I written unto you that believe on the name of the Son of God; that you may know that you have eternal life, and that you may believe on the name of the Son of God.* Again, *Verily, verily, I say unto you, He that heareth my word, and believeth on him that sent me, hath everlasting life, and shall not come into condemnation; but is passed from death unto life.*

— *Connect* —————————————

If you have never called upon His name according to the Scripture above, then do it right now.

JUST A THOUGHT...
Saved for sure, what a wonderful thought!

When You Have
No Place to Run
Psalm 142

September 11, 2001—the Twin Towers in New York City, the Pentagon in Washington DC, a hillside in Somerset County, PA, 2,996 persons were at ground zero with no place to run. On that memorable day, the war on terrorism was born.

The attack on America was issued by cowardly, immoral, evil, cruel, and sinful men. Men who are of the order of Satan, men who seek the stealing, destruction, and the killing of people. This work order came from hell to seize and to capture the souls of men. This war is active, and the file will not be closed till the neck of all enemies of God are under the sovereign foot of Jesus Christ.

I looked on my right hand, and beheld, but there was no man that would know me: refuge failed me; no man cared for my soul.

David, the "king-to-be" of Israel, was under the hunt by King Saul. David was found hunkering down inside a cave, hiding for the fear of his life. He was at a place where there was no place to run. The process of elimination had taken place. The exhausted recourses had run their course. His cry for help was intense. He was over his head in trouble and totally abandoned by men who were no longer found at his right side. Weakening moments, in solitary confinement, and in utter despair at the bottom of the world. David was brought very low and was in bad shape.

Cornered like a dog, David took refuge in his God. He poured his heart and soul out to God (2). A time when nothing is to be hidden, devastated in spirit, he tells all to the one who knows all. Our all-knowing God knows the path we are on. He is touched with the feelings of our infirmities, and is a very present help in a time of trouble. *When you have no place to run*, run to God; run to Him now and run to Him fast.

David began to pray, and pray with deep convictions (supplication). Praying with confidence that if this was the end of the day for him, having God was all he needed in life, no matter where life was. David said, *"You are my refuge, my portion in the land of the living."* If God was all you had, would He be enough? If you woke up one morning and all was taken, would you have anything left? *When you have no place to run but God,* is He enough shelter for you?

Paul had no place to run when he sang praises at midnight while in jail. Daniel had no place to run but to rest in the sheltering arms of God in a lions' den. Peter had no place to run, but got a good night's sleep in the wake of his head rolling the next day. Take refuge in God today as He unfolds His will for your life. Seek God and the Holy Scriptures to guide your life. The peace of God that passes all understanding will give quietness to the soul. The resurrection of Christ as our only hope will enable anyone to rise from any hellhole, being more than conquerors and triumphing over our greatest enemy—death.

—Connect—

At ground zero, having spent all that you have with every exit being closed, run to God; He will always provide a way of escape.

JUST A THOUGHT...
Praises unto God will lighten up any blackness of the night.

A Word Defining Cliff Hartley

Romans 7:14-16

For we know that the law is spiritual, but I am carnal, sold under sin. For what I am doing, I do not understand. For what I will to do, that I do not practice; but what I hate, that I do. If, then, I do what I will not to do, I agree with the law that it is good (NKJV). Paul said this about himself, but it sounds so much like me.

For some time after being saved, I thought when I sinned, I must not really be saved. But deep down inside there was a strong desire to do right, be right, and stay right. Little did I know then that there were two of me. One that was carnal and the other that was spiritual. With this being true, I'm convinced I'm saved beyond any shadow of a doubt, because God's ways are always contradicting my ways.

I asked an old preacher friend, Rev. Jerry Bruce, how long he had been a Christian. He said to me, *"Now, brother Cliff, if you had asked me how long I have been saved, I could tell you. But I'm only a Christian when I act like one."* That one word *"Christian"* is what I should be all the time, but it does not give definition about me. Saved and Christian are redundant terms in me, but not always.

I have been a student and in love with the Bible since 1963. For more than 40 years I have been studying, memorizing, and learning the Bible. Since 1975 I have made it a practice to read my Bible through at least once a year. This book tells me, if I love God, I will keep His commandments (I John 5). Being a lover of the Bible does not say very much about me when I'm disobedient to His Word.

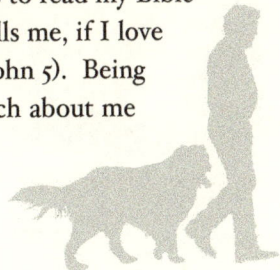

The term soul-winner is really what I want to be known for. However, it dawned on me one night after reading an obituary in the paper of a man who died that I was not much of a soul-winner, because I had failed to witness to him.

Nothing makes me more proud than for Jeanie to introduce me as her husband of more than 43 years, or my two sons, Brett or Todd, to say, *"This is my Dad."* There have been times that I have had to ask for their forgiveness. During those times it seemed being a husband or father had a hollow sound to it.

The word that defines Cliff Hartley more than being saved, a student of the Scriptures, a soul-winner, or a husband or father is the word: *"forgiven!"* Of all the inconsistencies found in my life, this one word remains constant—by the grace of God I stand forgiven of my sin that nailed Jesus to a cross. My sins have been hurled behind God's back. They have been cast in the depths of the sea. I have been forgiven of my iniquities and they are remembered no more. I have trusted the Gospel, repented of my sin, am covered by His blood, justified in the Spirit, and forgiven forevermore. So, when in the flesh I do those things which I hate, I rejoice in that His law contradicts my lifestyle. This alarm quickens the truth as to what I am: forgiven! What I am, I am by His grace and His forgiveness.

— *Connect* —

Forgiven, enough said!

JUST A THOUGHT...
What God has forgiven, He also has forgotten.

Worldwide Worship
Psalm 138

Worship takes on different forms as you witness *"religion"* taking place around the world from different cultures. Some will worship off of rough stumps in the wilderness while others will worship under refined steeples in metropolitan cities. Some believe in worship while some behave in worship. Some believe and behave in worship.

I know of no truer form of worshiping God than being part of the Lord's Supper service. There is no song, no homily, no setting that can move a person to react because of being in the divine presence of God like observing the bread and the contents of the cup from the Lord's table (I Cor. 11). When reminded that the body of our Lord was bruised beyond reorganization and His blood flowed down to the foot of the cross, covering any and all sin, nothing captures the heart as that does! One does not want to raise his hand here, he wants to remove his shoes.

"Real worship" changes a person. It is impossible to come into the presence of Deity and remain the same. Life will take on new meaning and old practices will pass away. It changes how we live, as always being with the one who is always with us. Worship is what we do 24/7, worshipers are who we are. The whole wide world needs to worship and experience God.

Worshiping God is a personal conviction that prompts a righteous conduct. David said, *"I will worship...,"* He also said, *"I will sing praise"* (1). This is worshiping God in spirit. He said, *"I will worship...thy name for thy truth"* (2). This is worshiping God in truth. David the king

worshiped God in prayer...and was strengthened in his soul. Something is very wrong when some are as sweet as sugar from 11 to noon on Sunday morning and behave like a devil on wheels throughout the week!

King David's desire was that all kings worldwide would worship God (4). There is coming a day when every knee will bow and every tongue will confess that He is Lord of lords and King of kings. Time will not change into eternity till every person who will ever enter heaven or hell will ascribe in spirit and in truth to the glory of the Lord.

What is God's reaction to true worship? Whether you sing praises to Him on top of a mountain or cry in the valley of the shadow of death, He will be with you (7). Responding to Him for who He is brings to Him the purpose for which we were created. Jesus said to the woman at the well, "*True worshipers shall worship the Father in spirit and in truth: for the Father seeks such to worship him. God is a Spirit: and they that worship him must worship him in spirit and in truth* (John 4:23). When the former things have passed away and all things become new, then we shall see His face, then we shall serve Him in one endless and ceaseless day, and then we shall reign with Him for ever and ever (Rev. 22:3-5). This is that which honors Him and glorifies Him. Then at that day, all of heaven and all of hell will know that God is God and there is none other. The whole wide world will know this truth.

— *Connect* —

Even though you are one, you are part of the whole wide world.
Honor Him today with...your presence before Him.

JUST A THOUGHT...
  Knees were made to bend; try bending them for Him.

XXXIX, Crown of a Champion
Revelation 3:11

Behold, I come quickly: hold that fast which thou hast, that no man take thy crown.

On Feb. 3, 2005, *USA Today* ran a cover sports page article on Barret Robbins, a 6' 3", 360-pound NFL football player who went AWOL two days before his team, the Oakland Raiders, would face the Tampa Bay Buccaneers in Super Bowl XXXVII. He went on a drinking binge to Tijuana, Mexico. The Bucs were crowned world champions, the Raiders lost, and Robbins forfeited his chance of playing in his biggest game of his career (and may have cost his team from winning the championship) and wearing pro sports' most coveted apparel—a Super Bowl Ring!

The New England Patriots squared off on the gridiron in Jacksonville, Florida, on Sunday, Feb. 6, 2005, against the Philadelphia Eagles in Super Bowl XXXIX. The Pats were crowned champions (their 3rd in 4 years—my team!) and winners of the 2004 season Super Bowl Ring.

A champion—there is no feeling like it, unless it happens more than once. Being crowned like such before the world, there are few who have experienced it. To achieve this most coveted ground, it takes years of hard disciplinary training, playing by the rules, and not quitting till the coronation day.

God will one day honor all those who have faithfully run the race, fought a good fight, kept the faith, and finished their course. God has laid up a crown for all those who love His appearing and have never taken their eyes off the goal.

The story of Haman versus Mordecai in the Book of Esther is of Super Bowl proportions. Haman sought

to be next to the king, wear his ring, adorned under the royal crown, and have all the people to reverence him. But when Mordecai refused to worship him as such, Haman in a rage built a hangman's noose for Mordecai, the Jew, and sought to destroy all of God's people. Under the providence of God, Haman was hanged on his own gallows, and Mordecai wore the coveted ring and was dressed in the royal garb with a great crown of gold.

To wear a crown is indicative as to who you are and the race you have won. It will clearly mark and set you aside from all others. Anyone can win, and the righteous judge who knows both the intent of the heart and the purpose to which you have been called will one day honor all champions.

There is an *incorruptible crown* (I Cor. 9:25) given by God that will last forever. It will be worth all the hard work one day. There is the *crown of life* (Jas. 1:12) promised by one who can not lie given to those who faced severe testing and endured unto the end. The *crown of rejoicing* (I Thess. 2:19) will be given to soul-winners of the Gospel. The *crown of righteousness* (2 Tim. 4:8) will be given to those who are players of the game and ready for the second coming of Christ. Then there is a crown for pastors, the *crown of glory* (I Pet. 5:4), given to pastors who are the personification of the chief Shepherd—the Lord Jesus Christ. These crowns are crowns of champions. They all will be cast at the feet of Him who sits alone on the throne, recognizing Him only as the Kings of king and Lord of lords. I can't wait till this victory happens. I will be there. What about you?

—Connect—

Even if all you can do is giving a cup of cold water in His name, you will not lose your reward.

JUST A THOUGHT...
Wasted years...never let it once be named about us.

The Fountain of Youth

I Timothy 4:12-16

The apostle Paul to Timothy: *"Let no man despise thy youth; but be thou an example of the believers, in word, in conversation, in charity, in spirit, in faith, in purity. Till I come, give attendance to reading, to exhortation, to doctrine. Neglect not the gift that is in thee, which was given thee by prophecy, with the laying on of the hands of the presbytery. Meditate upon these things; give thyself wholly to them; that thy profiting may appear to all. Take heed unto thyself, and unto the doctrine; continue in them: for in doing this thou shalt both save thyself, and them that hear thee."*

This is the true and real *fountain of youth,* if taken in, it will keep anyone spiritually young forever. *The fountain of youth* is not found in Florida, but in the Word of God.

Timothy forever lives as a young, dynamic superstar in God's Hall of Faith. In all the years we have read about him in the Bible, he is forever young in our minds, and the world today looks up to him. The process that led him to a worldwide stage was *Training the Trainer* by the apostle Paul. Paul was the mentor, young Timothy was the apprentice. Today, Timothy stands head and shoulders above his peers. He is the epitome of young people. Why?

Because of living a life of godliness. Staying godly never wears one out. Moses died being 120 years old, his eye was not dim nor his natural force abated. Joshua, at 80, climbed a mountain and claimed it for God. By following God's Word every day, our conduct, loving others, being alive spiritually, living by faith, and our example of virtues will show that our source is from an eternal fountain.

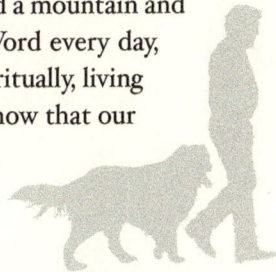

Timothy read a lot, was motivated by what he heard, and aligned himself with Scripture. He is measured by the people he met and the books which he read. *If he saw further than most men, it is because he stood on the shoulders of giants.* These never die; they read the same yesterday, today, and forever. He knew where to hang out and he always drank from wells that never ran dry.

He was gifted like any young person. However, unlike many young people, he never neglected his gift. He discovered his gift by making himself available. He developed his gift, investing his time. He dedicated his gift to the glory of God. What he did, he did with thanksgiving. He did it in the name of Jesus. He did it till the day he died. He treasured this gift and he never *withered on the vine.*

Timothy guarded these commands and never gave up on them. And by guarding these, he guarded himself from ever being a castaway. Joseph knew that the *pleasures of sin for a season* would bring an abrupt end to himself and others who needed him. A mighty oak tree which has grown for years can be cut to the ground in a blink of the eye, so is one that is filled with lust and the pride of life. The fountain from which we all drink will either be from the *water of life* or it will be from a cesspool of putrefaction.

—Connect—

There are a few good men who know how to follow through and finish well.

JUST A THOUGHT...
Think on these things and be forever young.

Jesus Speaks On Worry

Matthew 6:25-34

"Don't worry about one thing!" Sounds simple, doesn't it? Jesus is saying that if we would just stop and *smell the flowers* and consider how they grow, we would not worry about one single thing. Even the birds of the air, they do not sow or reap, yet the heavenly Father takes care of them. He says to all of us, we are more valuable than a whole world full of birds or lilies. Six times in this text, He uses the words: *"Take no thought."* Six times He is saying, *"Do not worry!"*

Here is a life-provoking principle—God is our heavenly Father and He is the King of the kingdom. All the cattle on a thousand hills belong to Him. He is the all-powerful God, big enough to care for each of us and 7 billion people just like us. Secondly, we are the servants of the almighty God. We are children of faith in the everlasting kingdom of God. When we are about our Father's business and seeking His kingdom first, then all the things which we will ever need will be supplied. To worry about "these things" is to act like what we were before we were born again—Gentiles, pagans, heathens!

The world knows of the JC Penney stores. Mr. JC Penney lost all of his worldly assets during the 1929 stock market crash. It made him so physically sick that he had to be hospitalized. One night he literally thought he was dying. He awoke only to hear the words of a song: *"God will take care of you, through every day, o'er all the way...."* He came to his senses, put things in priority, and the rest is history...JC Penney stores!

What is wrong with worry? Everything is wrong with worry. Note at least seven things:

1. Worry is worthless; it is no good.
2. Worry does not provide any answers to anything.
3. Worry will hinder the abundant and productive life as a Christian.
4. Worry will cause anxiety, and anxiety can cause sickness. Like a nervous breakdown!
5. Worry is a lack of faith, and a lack of faith is sin.
6. Worry will slow down the work of God.
7. Worry will break fellowship with God.

Now stop it! Stop worrying, *"for crying out loud!"* Start believing God to meet all your needs. David said, *I have never seen the righteous forsaken or his seed begging bread.* Lastly, *cast all your care on him, for he cares for you.* God is too kind and too wise not to give you the kindgom. We are His children, and it's His responsibility to see that we are taken care of. *Now, don't worry about one thing!*

— *Connect* —————————

Let us all admit that it is us, not God, that has the problem.

JUST A THOUGHT…
> *What will worry do for us today?*

It's All About Him

Matthew 25:31-46

Not everyone who says, Lord, Lord will enter into the kingdom, but they who will do the will of the Father. One day, Jesus will separate all nations of the earth as a shepherd will separate the sheep from the goats. Those nations who are believers and a friend to *"His brethren,"* the Jews, will enter into the kingdom of God. America, who is *"One Nation under God,"* has been blessed because of her loyal stand for God's people. She will be kept and will be protected because of God's promise.

When Israel was hungry and thirsty, we fed them. When they were strangers and sick, we gave them shelter. When they were naked and in prison, we extended to them companionship. There will come another time when the Jews will face strong persecution from a world dictator. And again, they will need help and support. And again, God-fearing nations like America will be there for them. Besides the tangibles, there is a deeper truth being unfurled, the tenderness to Christ, the Messiah. And for most of us, we are not even aware of it. But Jesus is and that is what will matter at the end of the day, because *"It's all about Him,"* not us!

America's saints are the sheep of His pasture. We are a giving people. We know how to give the *"widow's mite,"* we know how to restore like Zacchaeus, giving fourfold over and above. And as with the woman with the alabaster box, we give so generously. Even if it is only a boy's lunch—we will give and expect nothing in return. We give out of Christian virtues and out of the goodness of our hearts. Our giving is as unto the Lord. It's because *"It's all about Him!"*

We are the *"Good Samaritan"* of the world. We will set the sick on his own beast, carefully provide for them, and pay the bill. The response is from our hearts, the place where God looks. While others who have a "religious garb" will at times walk on the other side, leaving the stranger half dead, we will pour the oil of life into his wounds. It is God who has given unto us freely of all things. Given to us for what? Given to us, that we might freely give to others. *Inasmuch as we have done it unto the least, we have done it unto him.* "It's all about Him!"

We are commanded to give. Those who love God will keep His commandments. When we give, it's from a heart that is true and obedient. *We love God because he first loved us.* We love to give, and love to give cheerfully. This kind of giving will not go unrecognized. The little things which we do for others may pass over us as insignificant, but it will not pass over Him. We give because *"It's all about Him"* being the Savior of the world.

— *Connect* —————————
God wants the world to know all about Him.

Just a thought...
Do whatever as unto the Lord.

The Invitation of Jesus
Matthew 7:13-29

Jesus finished His famous Sermon on the

Mount with an *invitation*. After preaching about living by the laws in the kingdom's land, He closes His message by giving three final warnings. These warnings come with eternal judgment if there is failure to listen and to obey. There are consequences, as someone has said, *"Present choices determine eternal consequences."* The Bible says, *"Today is the accepted time; now is the day of salvation."* We must do now what one day we will be glad we've done when standing before God. When God calls, what matters is what we have done with Christ, His Son, the Savior of the world. What choice will you make? *Choose you this day whom you will serve.*

A super-lane highway is the road which all persons are traveling (13,14). This road is either northbound or southbound. The northbound is the narrow road; it leads to heaven. The southbound is the broad way; it leads to hell. Someone has defined this route as the narrow road (a difficult lane) going right up the middle of the broad way (an easy lane). The broad way has many travelers and it is a slippery slope which goes down to destruction. The southbound crowd is found going in the wrong direction. Repent of your sins today; God will change your direction.

Sheep and wolves are on this broad road (15-23). Jesus tells us to beware of wolves in sheep's clothing. They will tear us apart, and will spare none of the flock. Wolves in sheep's clothing: They look, walk, talk, act, and even their preaching sounds like they are sheep of the

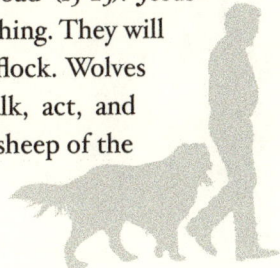

Lord's pasture...but they are not. These are from the devil's pack. There is something about them which just doesn't smell right! They are thugs from the religious ring, skimming off the top and feathering their own nest, profiteering from God's people. These are "sheep-killing wolves!" *My sheep know my name and they follow me.* Be alert which road you are traveling and which way the crowd is going.

Are you smart or a fool? Are you the wise man who built his house on a rock or the foolish man who built his house on the sand (24-27)? Will your house stand in the midst of the storm or will it collapse like a house of cards? Listen to Christ today; accept Him and come to Him now, just as you are. Softly and tenderly, He is calling you. Do not turn Him away!

— *Connect* —

*Christ is extending a personal
invitation to all who will follow Him.*

JUST A THOUGHT...
*And at the end of the day,
where will you be five minutes after you die?*

The Golden Rule
Matthew 7:1-12

The Golden Rule is not, "He that has the gold, rules." It is treating others as you want to be treated. Or doing to others with good intent before any good will ever come to you.

The power within the human heart is a powerful thing. The power which lies in the tongue is power unrestricted. If we put our mouth in gear before we put our minds in gear, we can do irreparable damage. There may not ever be the second chance to make that first impression.

We all have a testimony, feelings, integrity, character, and purpose in this world. Living by the Golden Rule will enhance and advance the cause of Christ for which He has called all believers to be engaged in. Selfishness in one's life will only delay the fulfillment of the work which He has committed to our trust. This is part of the Golden Rule!

Judge not; we are not Judge Judy! Unless...you are ready to be judged with the same standards for which you want to be judged. There is nothing wrong with judging, as long as we do it with a humble heart. If you are not ready to take the harsh, mean-spirited, ill-intended, critical words from friend or foe, then do not dish the same out. Be careful of the kettle calling the pot black. Judge with good and rightful judgment. Secondly, it may be that you can not see well to make good judgment. You may have a 2x4 stuck in your eye while trying to remove a speck of dust from your neighbor's eye. Do some personal heart-searching in your own life before trying to "straighten out" the mess in another. Live by the Golden Rule!

Learn how to give good things to others. It is more blessed to give than to receive. Living by the Golden Rule is listening to the often repeated request by others which comes to you. If you have a friend which keeps knocking at your door for three loaves of bread, get out of bed and give those to him. Learn how to ask God for things, then you will have patience when others put demands on your life. Giving a cup of poison when the request is for sugar is not the Golden Rule!

Do good, even if it hurts and costs you something. Living by the Golden Rule is not the plan of salvation. Just doing good will not get one to heaven. Only through the blood of Christ will anyone go to heaven. It is not of good works by which we are saved, only by His grace. However, men will judge us by our works. If you don't want your neighbor judging you because your garbage is scatterd in his yard, then buy a garbage can with a lid! Do well with good intent—live by the Golden Rule...you just may need a helping hand one day.

Connect

How nice and pleasant it would be if we all lived by the Golden Rule. Guess what...we will one day.

JUST A THOUGHT...
Do not lift your heel against your brother.

Alpha and Omega
Revelation 1:11

I am Alpha and Omega, the first and the last.... See Revelation 1:8, 21:6, and 22:13. This is in reference to God the Son (JESUS) being the first and the last. The name Alpha and Omega are the first and last letters in the Greek alphabet. JESUS is everything from A to Z. JESUS as well as God is sovereign. He has total control. He was and is the beginning and the end...and everything in between (the eternal one).

"Jesus is all the world to me"—what we mean by this is He is all that I will ever need in this life and the life to come. I can make it in any given situation, no matter what! There is no crisis that will ever happen in which He will not come to me and meet that specific need.

JESUS is my Savior. The greatest need in any person's life is a spiritual need, the need to be saved. We all are sinners in darkness, decay, and death. He has come to give life and light. The angel said He is the Savior unto all the world. He is the one who took my place on a cross where I should have been. He suffered my consequences and took my hell. My faith in His finished work has placed me in the family of God as a son of my heavenly Father. He has saved me from a life of hopelessness, heartache, and abandonment. And one day He will take me to heaven. *Alleluia, what a Savior!*

JESUS is my Shepherd. *The Lord is my shepherd, I shall not want.* Not only a shepherd but the good and chief Shepherd. He genuinely loves and cares for His sheep. We have all gone astray; we have turned every one to his own way. He has come to find us and to return us

to the fold. Sheep can lose their way quickly in this world. They have no idea where they are and can not find their way. During these times they are prey for the wolf, the bear, and the lion. He has promised to never leave us alone. *"Standing somewhere in the shadows, you will find Him."*

JESUS is our soon-coming King. *This is Jesus who was and is and is to come.* We like John will see a new heaven and a new earth coming down. He will dwell in us and we in Him. All tears will be wiped away. There will be no more troubled sea, neither death, sorrow, sadness, nor pain. The former things will vanish away.

I am Alpha and Omega, the beginning and the ending. The Alpha and the Omega is with us now and will be for all eternity.

— Connect —

"The King and I"—what an assured thought!
Oh, how I love Him.

JUST A THOUGHT…
Even so, come, Lord Jesus!

Visionaries
Proverbs 29:18

Without a vision, people perish.

I have never seen a discouraged person who has a vision. Vision here is what a person finds in the Word of God. The Word of God is a book of promises, peace, pardons, and a place in heaven one day. How could any live a life of defeat and discouragement?

A visionary is one who is committed, enthusiastic, excited, and passionate, and has an earnest desire for the things of God. He seeks first the kingdom of God. He is never out of sync, and has no remorse or regret. He will walk under every ladder and wait till every black cat crosses his path. He does not wait till his boat comes in. He is no pessimist or fatalist. He lives, walks, and behaves in faith. He believes in God!

When there is no vision of the Word of God, it means self-pity and ruin. Vision of the Word of God means contentment, satisfaction, and joy. A visionary has his vessel filled with oil, casting light in a dark place. He is Spirit filled and controlled. He is a living epistle known and read by men.

The Bible speaks about a person who brings salvation. His name is Jesus. There is no other name under heaven whereby men can be saved. When any sees this truth and responds in faith, he becomes a child of God. *Those who sat in a dark place saw a great light.* Refusing the Bible's plan of salvation means one will perish forever in hell and in outer darkness.

Happy is the man whose sin is covered by the blood. The Bible says, *We are justified by his blood.* The man

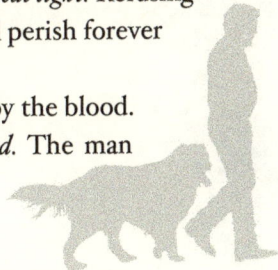

who lives by good works alone will have a rude awakening one day as he stands before God as a thief and a robber.

Vision will enable a believer to follow his Lord in baptism and church membership. Repent, be baptized, and forsake not the church. When there is obedience, there is peace. What if there were no place for you in a church to hear the preaching of the Word? People are destroyed for a lack of knowledge!

A visionary sees clearly this thing about tithing. He is happy that he has not robbed God. The tithe (10%) belongs to the Lord, not to the lottery. Give to God what belongs to Him and you will be happy that you did!

A man with a vision knows that the soul that sins will die. He believes there is a real hell and it is hot. He sees men lost and tries to pull them out of the fire. He knows the time is short. He knows Satan is seeking whom he may devour. His vision is clear, focused, and true.

— *Connect* —

One who keeps the law of God is a Bible student.

JUST A THOUGHT...
The Bible can provide 20/20 vision.

Borderline Christianity

Numbers 32

A mother was awakened in the middle of the night by the crying of one of her children. When she found him, he was lying on the floor almost under the bed. After calming him down and wiping tears, she said to him, *"Honey, the reason you fell out of bed was that you were sleeping too close to where you got in."* This is what is happening today with so many of God's children, they are sleeping too close to the edge where they got in—*borderline Christians.*

Moses' ultimate desire was to enter the land which flowed with milk and honey, the Promised Land, the utopia of the world. A land which God gave to the Jews under an irrevocable covenant. To his own demise, Moses only got to see the land, on the edge from Mt. Nebo, on the other side.

God gave this land to the children of Jacob, the twelve tribes of Israel. It belongs to them. However, the *children* of Reuben, Gad, and half of the tribe of Manasseh wanted to stay on the east side of God's chosen land. Moses may have responded with an *"I can't believe what I am hearing!"* It was a replay of history, the exact attitude of what their fathers had done forty years before. Many today are saying as these: *"Bring us not over Jordan,"* we would rather be pew warmers than having to place our hands to the plough. Borderline Christians they are!

After 40 years in the wilderness the only people who came out of Egypt to enter the land of Promise were Joshua, Caleb, and those younger than 20 years. These

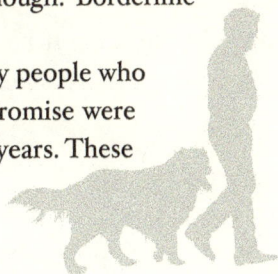

were the only ones who chose to go deeper into the land from where they entered. They were the ones seeking God's best, seeking God first, and seeking God's rest. Just getting into the land of blessings was not their only goal, they wanted the fullness of the land. Borderline Christians they were not!

Why would any who have witnessed God's provision and the recipients of God's promises, not want to go and have all that God only can give? Why would any want to stop short of God's divine mark for them? Some will choose the watered plains of the East and not choose the wealth from the Promised Land of God.

God will give us our request, He will let us choose what we want, He will let us live where we want to live, but it will bring leanness to our soul. We like Esau can sell our birthright for a mess of pottage. We like Lot can choose Sodom and lose our family. We either can have God's best or less than His best; it's our choice. We may rest on the edge but not without His safety.

Their interest was for the cattle (1) and for their little ones (16). So what if the price of gasoline goes to $6.00 a gallon? So what if we have another Katrina? So what if we are part of another 8.0 earthquake? So what if we have a WWIII? So what if we have 1.3 million Bird Flu Virus casualties? So what?! Our God is bigger than any fear and can answer any problem. God's hand will only lead to the light as we stay away from the edge.

—*Connect*—

Keep going deeper for God and you won't end up crying in the middle of the night as a borderline Christian!

JUST A THOUGHT...
Some are saved so as by fire.

What is God, Our Father, Like?

Matthew 5:48

"My dad has no equal, or peer, of any comparison. He is in a class all by himself. There is no person in all the world like my dad! My dad is perfect." That should be the expression from every boy or girl that has a loving daddy.

The most important person in all the world and in all the Bible is God. He bears many titles, but none is more personable for our understanding what He is like than "Father." It is a title which attracts the beholder, and when drawn to Him a new relationship is established. *But as many as received him, to them gave he power to become the sons (children) of God.* Now, it becomes *"Our Father,"* and we call him *"Abba"* Father. And with much respect and reverence it is as if we were to say, "Daddy!" It is only here that anyone will ever know what God is like. Anyone can know what God is like. He wants to be a Father to all of us.

He is always where I am. He has never and will never leave me alone. Dr. Jerry Falwell has said, *"He is nearer than the blood which courses through my veins or the air which fill my lungs."* The Bible says, *If I take the wings of the morning and fly to the uttermost parts of the world, behold, he is there. If I make my bed in hell, he is there.* What my Father is like more than anyone else is that, He is always there.

He knows my voice and my name. You never have to get His attention by telling Him who you are. He knows who you are and is waiting to hear from you. When you call upon Him, He understands you by the tone and sound of your voice. If you are hurting, He senses this so tenderly. He knows you by name, not by a social security number. The busy signal is never with Him, it most always is with us.

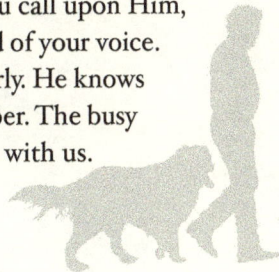

"This is my Father's world!" He created this world, and He has not stopped taking care of it. He is watching over His creation with a never-slumbering eye. You and I are part of that creation. It's the little details that make the big picture. We understand what He is like when we know He is *touched with the feelings of our infirmities. Poor little ole me* is so important to Him. That is just like my Father!

Personally, I was raised in a family of nine living children. My dad (Shade Hartley) treated us all the same. He was fair in his living and fair in his death. I can never say he loved the others more than he loved me. That is a little picture of what my Father-God is like. He loves all of us the same. Doesn't that make you feel important to Him?

Now, knowing what He is like, how could any of His children ever rebel or hurt Him? Want to make Him happy? Want to know what to give one who has everything? Open your heart and let Him live with you—do it now!

— *Connect* ——————

One must be born again into His family for Him to become your heavenly Father.

J UST A THOUGHT...
He is our everlasting Father and always will be.

What Will the Tribulation Days Be Like?

Mark 13:8

For nation shall rise against nation, and kingdom against kingdom: and there shall be earthquakes in divers places, and there shall be famines and troubles: these are the beginnings of sorrows. We all have faced some kind of trouble in our lives, times of deep anguish and heartaches. However, according to the Bible there is coming a time of sorrows which has not been since the beginning of time (Matt. 24:21). It is known in the Scriptures as the *tribulation* and with emphasis on the *great tribulation*. It will be the time of "wormwood"—bitterness, wrath, wickedness, woes, and great judgment without mixture of mercy or grace.

Bible scholars call it the time of *Jacob's Trouble,* the great day of God's wrath, or the time of great indignation. Theologically, it is the *seventieth week of Daniel's prophecy* (Dan. 9:24-27). A time period of seven years when the *"little horn,"* the antichrist, will come in peace. After three and one half years, this man of sin will be a man of great persecution. He will sit in the new temple and declare himself to be God. He is the incarnate Satan in the flesh, a terrorist of men.

From Rev. 6 through 18, the four horsemen will bring with them a flurry of great pain. This antichrist, this blasphemous beast of the sea, will rise only to induce a lawless lifestyle, defying the living God. He is called the *son of perdition, the man of sin,* and *the mystery of iniquity.* During this time *sin will reach unto heaven* (Rev. 18:5) and become

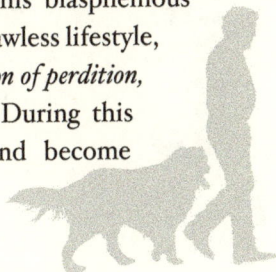

rampant in this world. He will control the social, financial, and the religious orders of the world. The famous "666" regulations will be enforced to buy or sell. Indeed a time of trouble from hell!

The Bible says these times will be so bad that men will seek death and will not find it. Times will be hard—it will take a full day's wage to buy one loaf of bread. One third of the trees will be burned up. Some say as many as 1.2 billion people will be killed. Pestilences will have unequaled epidemics.

There are a couple of good things which will happen. First, there will souls be saved which will have no number. These will be those saved in the tribulation days under the great preaching coming from 144,000 flaming evangelists. Those who like us will have been washed in the blood of the Lamb. Secondly, the coming of Christ with the mighty armies from heaven. Christ will put an end to this hellish activity at the close of the tribulation by being victorious in the battle of Armageddon. Satan will be incarcerated for 1,000 years and his cronies (the beast and the false prophet) will be cast alive into the lake of fire. Who shall be able to stand against the great day of God's wrath? Only those who have been washed and covered by the blood. Deliverance is yours now from this coming holocaust.

— Connect —

Your escape from this forthcoming horrible time is now.
Christ is the door for you to go through.

JUST A THOUGHT...
Sorrows upon sorrows will lace this time coming,
which is just ahead.

Saved at the Eleventh Hour

John 8:36

Very early on the *first day of the week,* Sunday, July 28, 2002, nine coal miners at the Quecreek Mine in Somerset, PA, were lifted one by one from a hellhole of total blackness, having been trapped with more than 60 million gallons of cold water up to their heads. When the telephone was dropped into that "bottomless pit," one of the rescue workers shouted, *"There's nine men who are ready to get the hell out of there. All nine are alive!"*

The workers, newscasters, coal riggers, a nation, and families were thankful, with much awaited smiles, as Randy Fogel, age 43, was the first to be lifted up in that safe yellow bucket. Eight more soon followed—all of them, not one was lost.

"I felt like being born again," either was said of these nine men, or something like that must have been expressed. Families must have felt that when seeing their husbands, daddies, relatives emerging from what could have been a watery grave for all of them, a second chance for these nine men.

As I sat and watched this, my thoughts ran much deeper than that "hellhole" which housed these nine men for several days. I was hurting for them, praying for them, and trusting Christ's power to deliver them. I was thinking of millions who like these nine men are trapped in a maze that seems to be hopelessly lost.

After three days of drilling and facing breakdowns, but with much perseverance, *"all nine men are alive"* and well today. And all the world can be free today as well.

This graphic occurrence which gripped the world is so exemplary of real lives who are trapped and in the

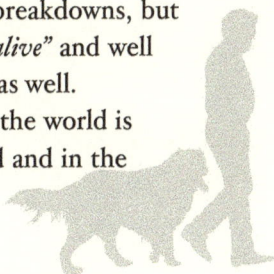

clutches of Satan. However, there is hope for every person that finds himself under the bars and chains of sin. That hope is Christ. He is the answer. The Scripture says, *"If the Son therefore shall make you free, you shall be free indeed"* (John 8:36).

Freedom, spiritual freedom, comes only from Jesus Christ. It is the acceptance of the truth which is in Him. *You shall know the truth* (Jesus is the truth), *and the truth shall set you free.* Christ can free one, nine, or the entire world.

John Wesley wrote: *"Long my imprisoned spirit lay, fast bound in sin and nature's night; Thine eye diffused a quick'ning ray, I woke, the dungeon flamed with light; My chains fell off, my heart was free; I rose, went forth, and followed thee."*

— Connect —
Are you ready to be free today?
Trust Christ and His truth; it's your only hope!

JUST A THOUGHT...
There is no way out of a "grave" situation,
unless it comes from above!

The Great White Throne Judgment

Revelation 20:11-15

And I saw a great white throne, and him that sat on it, from whose face the earth and the heaven fled away; and there was found no place for them. And I saw the dead, small and great, stand before God; and the books were opened: and another book was opened, which is the book of life: and the dead were judged out of those things which were written in the books, according to their works. And the sea gave up the dead which were in it; and death and hell delivered up the dead which were in them: and they were judged every man according to their works. And death and hell were cast into the lake of fire. This is the second death. And whosoever was not found written in the book of life was cast into the lake of fire (Rev. 20:11-15).

Make no mistake about it, the Bible records a time coming when Christ will judge the *"dead, small and great"* as they stand before Him at the *"Great White Throne Judgment!"* Christ will be the Supreme Judge and He will be rendering judgment from the records of documents of every person at this judgment and everything in the lives of those who will stand before him on this fearful and fatal day. *"The Father has committed all judgment unto the Son."*

"The dead, small and great." These are the lost whose names are not found in the book of life, and no record is given of their spiritual birth.

"...and the books were opened...!" Books which have been written on each of us since the accountability

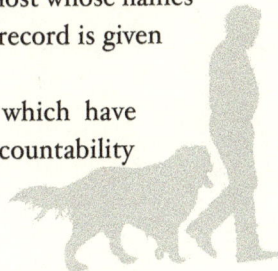

of our sin. Books which record our deeds, thoughts, actions, words, and our secrets. All of it will be exposed and documented on this day. These will be judged according to their works which have been written in the books.

"...and another book was opened, which is the book of life." The book of life which records the names of all those who will go to heaven. Those standing at the Great White Throne Judgment will not have their names recorded. Why? They have been blotted out. Their names (I believe) were once recorded by God for all one day to go to heaven, but having lived and spurned the grace of God, rejecting His Son Jesus Christ over and over, having never been born again, these will have their names stricken from the record. There was never a time of trusting Christ as their Savior. Now, at the Great White Throne Judgment, they face a Savior who is now their judge, whose gavel comes down in their presence with the sound of a trumpet turning the wicked into hell and the eternal lake of fire.

— Connect —

Jesus will say at that day, "Depart from me,
I never knew you." Here never means never!

JUST A THOUGHT...
This is not a place anyone wants to stand at the end of the day!

How to Embrace the Suffering

Romans 12:15

Rejoice with them that do rejoice, and weep with them that weep.

How does one get his arms around some 400,000 persons left homeless and jobless after Hurricane Katrina hit the southern part of the Gulf States on Monday morning, August 29, 2005, with gusts of winds up to 165 mph and leveled buildings as if they were a house of cards? What can one do when facing damages up to 125 billion dollars in cost, a putrid of human corpses found everywhere, and streets flooded with toxic and human waste up to the gutters of housetops? Where does one go to help tens of thousands who are suffering to the point that life as they knew it will never be the same? Why does one feel so helpless in trying to lift a burden in which no one can bear? When will the tears stop flooding our faces? When will we begin to rejoice again with them that once knew how to rejoice?

Disasters like this are not new to America. We wept with them that wept when Pearl Harbor was attacked by the Japanese on December 7, 1941. We wept with them that wept when terrorists struck the Pentagon, crashed a plane on a hillside in Pennsylvania, and took towers down to rubble in New York City on...September 11, 2001. We are weeping with those who are weeping whose lives have been raped by Hurricane Katrina.

So, just how does one embrace those whose lives are filled with agony, misery, and pain? Here are a couple of things anyone with a broken heart can do.

We can pray. It may sound shallow, yet the resources are as deep as the ocean and as high as the heavens.

The Bible teaches that *the effectual fervent prayer of a (one) righteous man availeth much* (James 5). Nothing is impossible when one person, right with God, is on his knees in prayer. Faith and believing in God that is as small as a grain of mustard seed will remove mountains and recover any loss. Those who are hurting are crying out, *"Brethren, pray for us."* Prayer is what we will do, prayer is what we must do, but that is not all that we will do.

When you pray, say, *"Father, bring those who are hurting, who have lost loved ones, who have no homes to go back to, into your presence and let revival sweep America from coast to coast."* While many may have been lost in the storm, pray that many will find Christ as their personal Savior. Ask God that this *Tower of Siloam* may spur a spiritual awakening unlike we have ever seen. Like Christ, weep over America.

Join a group. Let me recommend to you that you can do more than just pray; you can send money. (Preachers have no problem asking for money!) A group that I am most familiar with and trust highly is the *Southern Baptist Disaster Relief* effort program. You can send money on-line by going to: www.namb.net/dr. While you may not be able to go physically, you can go by sending financial aid. When on-line, your giving reaches destination points immediately when disaster strikes. Giving represents a weeping heart. Weeping moves people to action. Do it now!

— Connect

*Take heart, never is there a bucketful of water
that can not take on one more drop. Your drop along with a million
or so adds up. Pray as if everything depends on God and work as
if everything depends on you. They will feel your warmth.*

J ust a thought...
Prayer changes the heart first.

A New Day With
New Definitions
Proverbs 22:28

Remove not the ancient landmarks which thy fathers have set (Prov. 22:28).

The definition of an oxymoron: a rhetorical figure in which incongruous or contradictory terms are combined. Example: Removing the Ten Commandments from the courthouse while making people swear to tell the truth, the whole truth and nothing but the truth, so help you God...while placing your hand on the Bible!

When Moses served the Lord, the people followed him. When Joshua served the Lord, the people followed him. Then the Bible says in Judges 2:10—*and there arose another generation after them which knew not the Lord, nor yet the works which he had done before them.* In one generation, there were a people who went into idolatry and serving other gods! What?!

This is a new day of redefining values that have made our lives safe and secure for so long. God made them male and female once upon a time. Now you can be whatever you want to be. Gender has no rule these days. The first institution was between one man and one woman. Yet in this new day, thousands of gay and lesbian couples are being married in matrimony. I wonder what rage would surface if the Statue of Liberty were replaced with Ozzie Osbourne! Would anyone notice or care?

In the beginning God created the heavens and the earth... in six days. We have a generation who has believed the devil's lie that it took billions of years to form

and fashion the earth. Darwin, with his evil black box, has become the textbook about God—I say baloney! God told Adam and Eve to be fruitful and to replenish the earth. How in this world can two people of the same sex do that between themselves? Would someone get me into a house before the sky falls on my head if that can happen?

Our fathers have taught us what their fathers have taught them. Generations after generations, we have had fathers who trusted in God, were tested by God, whose testimonies have been rock solid, and who have taught the difference between right and wrong. The new day has produced a generation which now curse their mother and father. A wicked and adulterous generation is coming. Look out, they are nearer than you believe.

We are defining the words *kill and murder* and replacing them with abortion. We have changed the word drunk to alcoholic. We have replaced the Ten Commandments with political correctness. Life, liberty, and the pursuit of happiness is being threatened by a socialistic government which will regulate both the cow and the milk.

Before God blows the light out on this candlestick, there needs to be a generation that will come back to the Bible and believe it as God's Word from cover to cover. Listen to what our fathers are saying. They may be old, but they are wise. And one other thing, leave the landmarks alone. They will define you who you are, where you have come from, and where you are going. Ask the new kid on the block if he knows that. Dah!

Connect

If we draw nigh to God, he will draw nigh to us.

JUST A THOUGHT...

Remember the good old days when kids used to say "Yes ma'am and yes, sir," when Mom would not allow us to burn trash on Sunday, and if we got a whipping in school, there was one waiting for us at home?

The Eradication of Evil Men
Psalm 140

Terrorists attacked a school in Ossetia, Russia, leaving 340 dead—156 of these were children. President George Bush gave an example of Muslim men who stood in his office with their right hands severed under the brutal regime of Saddam Hussein. Since 1973 an estimate of 45 million unborn babies have been slaughtered in their mother's womb by abortion.

Seven billion people all over this world want freedom, liberty, and free enterprise. They want to live a quiet, peaceful, and a reasonable life. Yet from the earliest of manuscripts and records there have been evil men who are the epitome of the man of sin who seeks the stealing, destruction, and the killing of the innocent. Will there ever come a day when this world will be purged from wicked men? Yes, a day is coming when all tears will be wiped away.

Pharaoh made Jews live unbearable lives. Nebuchadnezzar would throw men into a furnace of fire to satisfy his selfish desires. Herod would murder babies and behead men of God like John the Baptist to bolster his pride. Pilate, that flimsy, milk toast back-boned piece of human flesh, was afraid to take a stand for the Son of God and ordered Him crucified on a cross. All of these and millions like these have been, and still are, driven with the disposition of Satan himself. They are alive and in place in carrying out the whims and the intent of this antichrist, this devil, this wicked, this hateful and violent mind which is corrupt.

The Bible is clear in their description—they are wicked. They are for bloodshed, their words are filled

with the poison like that coming from an adder's tongue. They will sit atop of dead men's bones at any cost. They are wrong, and one day they will all be exterminated, obliterated, annihilated, and destroyed. Hallelujah!

Until that day comes, pray like mad. Cry out to God, He is touched with the feelings of our infirmities. Our God is our strength who enables us with the gift of grace to encounter the severest of attacks. Pray for the salvation of this kind of deranged minds. Pray the Lord's Prayer every day on your behalf and the behalf of others who are under the control of wicked men: *"Deliver us from evil."* Pray for the "evil speakers" to be purged.

Be patient. Know this that the Lord will maintain the cause of the afflicted. God is fattening these hellish leaders for a hog-killing day (James 5). Their miseries will be a thousandfold returned. And these filthy, Satan-deceived puppets will be overthrown and cast into the lake of fire forever, along with him and his cronies. *Be patient unto the coming of the day of the Lord.*

This world is run by many who are sinful, cruel, evil, and have proud minds. They will fall, and will be cast into flaming pits, never to rise again. The eradication of evil men will indeed come, their purpose will smoke forever as a witness against them, and their abomination will never be heard of again.

— Connect —

Let the peace and the promises of God establish your hearts of faith. One day the righteous will bow to give thanks and will be forever without sufferings and dwell in the presence of the Lord.

JUST A THOUGHT...
The former things are passed away!

Christianity 24/7

Jesus saith unto him, I am the way, the truth, and the life: no man cometh unto the Father, but by me (John 14:6).

The epitome of Christianity is Jesus Christ. He is all the word Christianity can ever mean. He spoke of Himself being the only way (not some way) to God—"*I am the way.*" He is the total personification of truth (not some part of truth); there is no truth apart from him—"*I am the truth.*" And He is the center of life (not just a life); there is no life apart from him—"*I am the life.*" He is the divine incarnation of God Himself who came in a body prepared by God, written in the volume of the book of God, and to do the will of God. Jesus Christ is God's only begotten Son who came to suffer on a cross, to die a criminal's death, and to rise victoriously over sin, death, Satan, and the grave. Apart from Him, there is no such thing as a Christian, there is no power to please God, and there is no hope or promise of heaven for anyone.

Jerry Vines said once, *"Our churches are in trouble today. There is virtually no difference between the average church member and the person who is not a Christian. God meant for the Christian to be different, to live a different kind of life, and to be on a different moral level from those who are not Christians. And yet, there is practically no difference in lifestyle."* Someone else has remarked, *"We church members are often like the farmer's well that freezes up in the winter and dries up in the summer."* Jesus said, *"Ye call me Master and Lord: and ye say well; for so I am"* (John 13:13). *"And why call ye me, Lord, Lord, and do not the things which I say"* (Luke 6:46)?

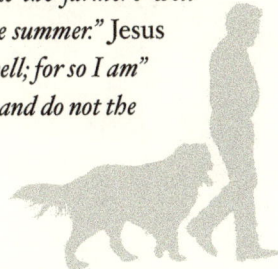

Let me address some things which should be part of the Christian life 24/7. We are worshipers of God, and worship is what Christians do. We can worship Him every second of our lives in spirit and in truth. Nothing should ever keep us from reverencing God. Eleven A.M. to noon on Sunday mornings is not the only hour that this can be done. The breath of the Christian is prayer. The Bible says we are to pray without ceasing and also to give thanks for everything. Prayer can accept anything that comes into our lives. There is only one thing that will stop prayer and that is sin. *"If I regard sin in my heart, the Lord will not hear me. Nothing lies beyond the reach of prayer except that which lies beyond the will of God. Prayer can do anything; prayer is omnipotent" (Torrey).*

The ability to give is a gift that God gives that we might give to others. *It is more blessed to give than to receive.* The 24/7 Christian always has something to give. Praising the Lord is that which should be part of our communication every day. Since God is everywhere, and there is not a spot where He is not—*praise Him!* Sinners for whom Jesus died stand shoulder to shoulder and eye to eye with us 24/7. We have the Gospel to give to them. And *greater is he that is in you than he that is in the world*...24/7! You can live for God 24/7, overcome the devil 24/7, and enjoy the Christian life...24/7. You really can!

— *Connect* —

Being found in Him by way of new birth, anyone can live the Christian life, have the abundance of life every day, walk in the power of the Holy Spirit, and please God by faith...24/7!

JUST A THOUGHT...
The Father seeks true worshipers to worship Him.

Unto Us a Son is Given

Isaiah 9:6

One of the busiest days of the year in the
marketplace is the day after Christmas. Two
reasons: one for sales, the other for returns. Taking back
things which don't fit, finding a replacement, or some rather having the
money than the gift.

What to buy today for others is difficult. People in America seem
to be loaded with the abundance in their lives. And when we do, the
bearing and sharing gifts to one another comes in multiple variations.

Do you know of anything which brings more joy than the time
when a baby is born into a family? There is none. It is a time of family
gatherings, and news of the baby travels far and wide and conversations
develop like no other time. Is it a boy or a girl? Does he/she have all his/
her fingers and toes? What did you name the baby? How much did he/
she weigh? What can I buy for him/her?

I want you to consider the gift that God Himself would select when
giving to people. The gift would be the ultimate and superior, and would
be for a lifetime. One that would meet needs, bring immediate joy, and
one that would be the best. That gift: His only begotten Son! *"Unto us a
Son is given..."* Trivia—do you know how much Jesus weighed when He
was born? I will have the answer to that question in my next musing.

God's Son was not born, but He was given. God gave
Him to the world as a child, an infant baby. Like us in
the natural, there was a time and a place for His birth.
But so much unlike us, His birth was miraculous.
Conceived and born in a virgin womb. *And she was*

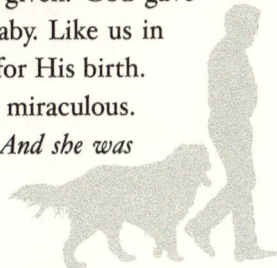

found with child, before they came together, of the Holy Ghost. The Bible says that Jesus was born of a virgin: *Behold a virgin shall be with child.* When God gave us His Son, He settled the question when life begins. Framers of abortion ask the question: When does life begin? When can it begin but at conception. There was a time when JESUS was born, but never a time when JESUS was not God's Son, even while being carried for nine months in His mother's womb!

And this Son came for a purpose—for the salvation of the lost. He would be the sacrifice and a Savior. *And she shall bring forth a Son, and thou shalt call his name JESUS; for he shall save his people from their sins. Born unto you this day, a Savior, which is Christ the Lord. Unto us a Son is given,* with a name unlike any other name, the only name whereby men are saved! There would be no other gift like unto God's Son, which would bring peace and joy to all!

Unto us a Son is given... This was the Son of God and God-the-Son Himself coming in the flesh. The great doctrine of the incarnation was introduced to the world. *The Word became flesh and dwelt among us...* as then and now and forever will be, with a body. They called Him *Emmanuel—God with us.*

— *Connect* —

Is there anyone who has ever received a gift that has not shared that gift with others. Some may cross your path who have never experienced the news of this Son of God, the Savior of the world.

J U S T A T H O U G H T ...
God in the flesh with nail prints in His hands—how could any gift bring more joy?!

Unto Us a Child is Born

Isaiah 9:6

The prophet spoke of His birth 700 years before He was born, and an angel announced His birth. He was born from a virgin's womb, wrapped in swaddling clothes, fed from His mother's breast, cradled in a manger bedded down with straw, and shepherds gave witness thereto. *A child is born...unto you this day...!*

Jesus was born the first time some 2,000 years ago in Bethlehem. He will be born the second time to the Jews, when they shall see Him at the second coming, when *they will look upon him whom they pierced.* At this time, a nation will be born in a day. And more so, He can be born again anytime, anywhere to anyone by grace through faith. He can be conceived in a heart as He was in a womb.

This child born unto us has been set for the rise or fall of all men. By His birth, His life, and His death will all men be judged. This child was not born to live in some royal garb, but to die in a rich man's grave. This child was born indeed and we cannot explain it away. A day is coming when all men will bow and confess the truth about this child.

Unto us a child is born that we might know Him. *And she brought forth her firstborn son and wrapped him in swaddling clothes.* This child's birth was witnessed by lowly shepherds, who said, *"Let us go and see this which the Lord has made known unto us."* In John 1:14 it says, *And the Word was made flesh and dwelt among us, and we beheld his glory.* This child born unto us was God manifested in the flesh— *Emmanuel, God with us.* We who have seen this child in the flesh, have seen the Father, and we know we are of God and are known of God.

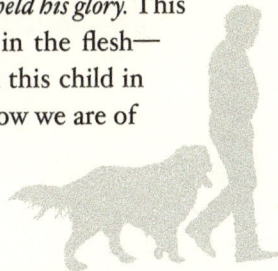

Unto us a child is born that we might grow in Him. The *tidings of great joy have been made available to every person. This child born unto us was the true Light which lighteth every man that is come into the world.* We no longer grope in darkness, but we grow in the light of the world—JESUS. By saving faith in the Son of God we have taken in His flesh and His blood. Living by faith as newborn babes, we have a craving desire for the Word of God, that we may grow thereby. *This child born unto us* enables us to *grow in grace and knowledge. This child born unto us is the way, the truth, and the life* which will guide us on our journey.

Unto us a child is born that we might show Him unto the world. The shepherds when they came and saw, *made known abroad the saying concerning this child. And they returned, glorifying and praising God for all the things that they had seen as it was told them.*

— Connect

*What an opportunity this Christmas season brings to believers—
there is no better time of the year to preach Christ unto the
world than this time. Soul-winning season is any time, but never
more ripe than this season. The people are never
more ready to hear than this time of the year.*

JUST A THOUGHT...
*Oh, I almost forgot. Trivia—how much did Jesus weigh when
He was born? His weight was the weight of the sin of the world.
And the Lord laid on Him the iniquity of us all!*

The Foursquare Church

Psalm 122

I was glad when they said unto me, Let us go into the house of the LORD. Our feet shall stand within thy gates, O Jerusalem. Jerusalem is builded as a city that is compact together: Whither the tribes go up, the tribes of the LORD, unto the testimony of Israel, to give thanks unto the name of the LORD. For there are set thrones of judgment, the thrones of the house of David. Pray for the peace of Jerusalem: they shall prosper that love thee. Peace be within thy walls, and prosperity within thy palaces. For my brethren and companions' sakes, I will now say, Peace be within thee. Because of the house of the LORD our God I will seek thy good.

Since the day of my conception into the family of God (Fall of 1955), I have been part of no denomination other than the Baptist. I was Baptist born and Baptist bred, and when I die, I will be Baptist dead! However, I have some dear friends that are serving God with a life of integrity and a sincere heart that are part of a *Foursquare Church*. We are in the same church, but sitting on different pews.

You should feel comfortable in your church. I'm not speaking about plush carpet and padded pews. You should be secure in what your head is listening to and how that transcends into your heart and everyday living. You and I are what we eat.

Square one of a Foursquare Church: You and your church should always have a compassion flowing from a burning heart to reach souls for Christ. Here is a question for you: Is there anyone in your life whom you have led to Christ and brought to your church? Is there anyone

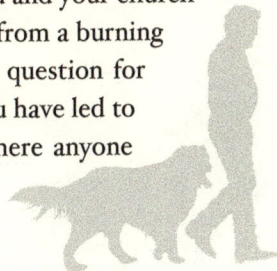

that can say, "*I was glad when they* (you and me) *said unto me, 'Let us go into the house of the Lord?'*" If you hesitated with that question more than three seconds, most likely there are not.

Square two: You and your church should be indoctrinated with the Word of God. Lives are changed not by environment, but by the Word of God. When your feet are squarely standing in the right place, it will produce a life *compacted together,* without schisms and not shaken by every wind of doctrine.

Square three: Jesus said, "*My house shall be called a house of prayer.*" The Father's business is not standing on the outside selling junk on the parking lot, but kneeling on the inside in prayer. You will have no doubt that you are in the right church by the peace of God that follows prayer.

Square four: *Because of the house of the Lord our God I will seek thy good.* The apathy in our heads means a lukewarm heart. Many are found in the pews, but few are laboring for the good of God.

— *Connect* —

God's good is only found when you seek Him with all (mind, body, soul, and spirit) your heart. A Foursquare Church stands securely, will not falter, will not faint, and will not fail.

JUST A THOUGHT...

Peace rules.

Civanna Carlene Christian

John 11:25,26

On September 1, 2006, we buried little
Civanna Carlene Christian, a beautiful, bubbly,
bouncing three-year-old. Her life in this life ended instantly
as she was tragically killed by an oncoming vehicle, but immediately
began living an endless life in the presence of our heavenly Father. She
is now what her parents ever wanted her to be—all grown up and living
the abundant life in heaven. She is more alive now than she has ever
been. She is and will be sadly missed by a loving family who had her, so
many friends who knew her, and a church that loved her. Yet, she was
gladly received by those in heaven who went on before her, waiting to
welcome her to her new home.

Jesus said, *"Whosoever liveth and believeth in me shall never die."* Children
of the Father never die! Oh, there may be this light and brief appointment
of departure (death) which we all must meet in this life, but there is no
end of living. Death will be swallowed up in victory when this corruption
has put on incorruption and this mortal has put on immortality. Death
has no sting and the grave has no victory for those who have made their
peace with God and have made preparations when this *dust shall return
to dust.* Jesus also said, *"I am the resurrection and the life: he that believeth in
me, though he were dead, yet shall he live."* He said again, *"Whoso findeth
me, findeth life."* Christ, who now resides at the right hand of
the heavenly Father, is our life.

God offers only life. He has made life available to
everyone, not death. This life is Jesus Christ. He has
set before all men, life and death; it is up to each of us

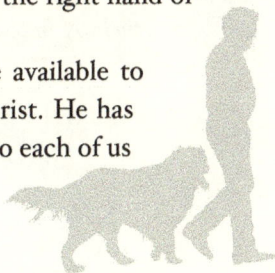

to choose life. By not choosing Christ, you automatically have chosen death. When you choose life, you choose Christ, who is life, our life. He said, *"I am...the life."* There is no way besides His way, there is no truth besides His truth, and there is no life besides His life—none whatsoever! He is not just a way; He is the only way, He is not just a truth, He is the only truth; and He is not just a life, He is the only life. Being found in Him and His presence, there is no death, only life and life everlasting. This is the very reason the Scriptures say, *I shall not die...* What that means to me is not now, not ever!

It is not the will of your Father that one of these little ones perish. Some have said, *"Well, it was just Civanna's time to die!"* No, it was not! We live in a very cruel, sinful, evil, painful, and hurtful world. Living here below we have our times of tears and heartaches. Until that day when we awake in His presence and likeness, that day when all tears will be wiped away, we live with sorrowful events, sickness, and hurt. Lazarus, Jesus' friend, got sick!

"The other children will take Civanna's place." No, they can not. Mary and Martha did not take Lazarus' place—they wept and missed him! Lazarus, Jesus' friend, was buried.

Others may have said, *"God wanted Civanna more than her parents did."* No, He did not. *Children are an heritage and a gift from the Lord.* Children are a blessing to us here in this world. God has no desire to take your children away from you. His desire is that you enjoy His gifts as long as you live in this world. Lazarus, Jesus' friend, came from the grave!

"Whosoever liveth and believeth in me shall never die." Jesus said, *"Do you believe this?"*

— *Connect* —

There is no hurt in this life like the hurt of a loss of a child.

JUST A THOUGHT...
A child shall lead them!

The Congregation of the Saints
Psalm 149

A woman was asked by a co-worker, *"What is it like to be a Christian?"* The co-worker replied, *"It is like being a pumpkin. God picks you from the patch, brings you in, and washes all the dirt off of you. Then He cuts off the top and scoops out all the yucky stuff. He removes the seeds of doubt, hate, greed, etc. Then He carves you a new smiling face and puts His light inside of you to shine for all the world to see"* (Forward/Sidel).

If any man be in Christ, he is a new creature; old things are passed away; behold, all things are become new. When a person becomes a believer in Christ, he is by way of definition a saint. One who follows the example of Christ through indwelling and leading of the Holy Spirit of God. Paul wrote to the church of God at Corinth, those who were sanctified in Christ, *called to be saints...*(I Cor. 1:2). A saint that is joined to a congregation (a called-out body) has been called to be obedient in fulfilling God's will and reaching this world for Christ. Life in the congregation of the saints as it is known takes on new dimensions, purpose, and conformity.

This congregation therefore is the Lord's people of whom He takes great pleasure in. And I do too—there is no better company in the entire world that I would rather be with than God's people. He cut the pattern, cast the die in the image of His Son, and offered this new and better way to whosoever will. What we become in Him, we give Him glory. We are made in Him and His likeness, we move in Him and have our being, and we mimic Him in our behavior. They took notice of His disciples as they walked the streets of Jerusalem, that they had been with Jesus!

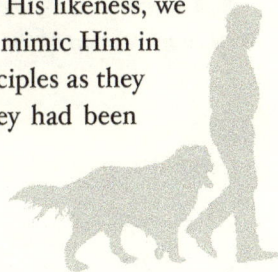

The congregation of saints—number one, they love to sing the praises of the Lord. We are a happy bunch, happy that we are saved and happy of going to heaven one day. We get excited about our new life, and brother, does it ever show! God has no secret saints or grandchildren. We express what we have in our hearts by singing. We sing joyfully and we sing loud. We've got something to sing about today. When a man knows how to sing a new song unto the Lord, he is happier, and everyone around him is better off. Singing makes one want to dance as he listens to the timbrel and the harp. You feel better by tapping your feet to a good and new song! *Sing unto the LORD a new song, and his praise in the congregation of saints.*

Secondly, *the congregation of the saints* knows how to execute the two-edged sword of the Spirit. We know how to wield the weaponry of the Scriptures and hold others accountable to *thus saith the Lord.* Heads of state become speechless and are as they were in chains of iron when confronted with the power of the Word. This sword has been honed, it is ready for use, and is used skillfully to cut to the quick of the matter. There is no greater or stronger voice from any block of people than that of *the congregation of the saints* who knows the power of the two-edged sword. *Let the high praises of God be in their mouth, and a two-edged sword in their hand...*

— *Connect* —

One day the congregation of the saints will sing together in that great heavenly choir unto the Lord, and sing before the one who sits on a throne. Hallelujah, what a day that will be! I can't wait!

J UST A THOUGHT...
The congregation of the saints are expressive and they execute.

The Impulsive Denial

Mark 14:66-72

Question number one: Could you ever deny the Lord Jesus Christ as your personal Savior? You may have said both publicly as well as in the quietness of your heart, "I love my Lord and I will love Him to the end." Know what? I really believe you do. Question number two: Have you ever denied your Lord? If you are like me, the answer is quick and without hesitation—ashamedly so, but transparently honest: yes! Oh, how I wish it were not so. Lastly: What was your response and how did that change your lifestyle? If it has helped you, I would like to know about it. Take a moment and write me a note about your story. Peter did and look how it has helped millions!

Chuck Colson—the *"hatchet man,"* who would go to any depths for the sake of his party and his love for the late President Richard Nixon, denied everything until he could go no further—until in 1974, when he confessed to his role in the Watergate charges and was sentenced to prison for a term of three years. However, when he came out of prison, he was a changed man. Today under his direction of the *Prison Fellowship Ministries,* which is worldwide, he is helping hundreds of thousands of inmates and their families to find Christ, adjust to bad situations, and find purpose in life. *The Boston Globe* reported: *"If Mr. Colson can repent of his sins, there has to be hope for everybody."* Amen!

Peter, the prince of the apostles, the leader of the pack, and many times the spokesperson for the others recklessly denied his Lord, not only once, but three times! How could that ever have happened to the

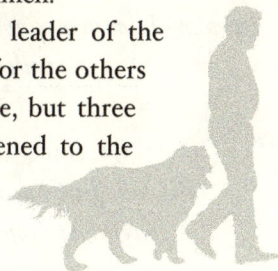

man who once said he would lay his life down for his Master. The one who said, though all men will forsake Him, yet he would not, but he did. The man who walked where no other man ever walked with His lord...on water! This man, had it not been for Jesus healing Malchus' ear, would have gone to the cross for his impulsive action in the Garden of Gethsemane. Although this man followed his Lord afar off, yet his desire was to be closer than any other. And as close as he was, yet in this time of his life he was so far away. In his heart he would die defending Christ, yet his record reads of an *impulsive denial*—three times.

His presence at the trial shows his courage and his interest; however, the pressure of his denials led to his weakness. The man who swung the sword would not want to show his face where he could have been arrested, were it not for his loyalty to his Lord. There is a breaking point in all of us, and sad to say, the other life in all of us emerges at the worst of times. To add fuel to the flame, Christ sent a burning ember of fire right through the heart of Peter when He (Christ) turned and looked upon him (Luke 22:61). When the rooster went *"cock-a-doodle-doo"* for the second time, it buckled the legs of Peter into a sorrowful, sobbing repentance. Peter struck out as he remembered the words of Christ.

We do not hear of Peter again till...after the Lord's resurrection, when Jesus told the women to tell His disciples and...Peter. Peter went back to his fishing business and guess who shows up for breakfast? After dining, Jesus asked Peter three times, "Lovest thou me?" Three times Peter said, *"Lord, I love you."* Jesus said to Peter, *"Feed my lambs."* It was Peter who gave the keynote address on the day of Pentecost where 3,000 conversions took place.

— *Connect* —

*Remember your impulsive denials when you have denied
knowing Him in a crowd, when your lifestyle creates questions.
It will cause you to weep too!*

JUST A THOUGHT...
*God will give you a second chance and more if needed
to return to your old self of love and devotion.*

The Incomparable Christ

Mark 16

Would you let a traitor embrace you with a hypocritical gesture of affection? Could you remain silent when bogus lies are forged and fabricated against you right before your eyes? How would you react if you were within hearing distance listening to your most ardent follower deny he ever knew who you were? If you knew you were going to be flogged and lacerated from the crown of your head to the soles of your feet, could you go through with it? Would you feel like committing suicide ahead of time if you knew you were going to die in a humiliating open forum as a foul-mouth thief? And do you think you could keep your sanity knowing you would be abandoned and totally forsaken by family, friends, and even God almighty? Well, could you?

Let me answer all those questions without hesitation for you. The answer is no, not one! But wait a second, my friend, there is one who would, could, and should—Jesus, the supreme sacrificial Lamb of God, the one who was slain before the foundation of the world. He drank the bitter cup filled with the wrath of God without compromise or failure. What you, me, or seven billion like you and me could not do, He did in the will of the Father so we can experience the peace of God which passes all understanding.

No one can dismiss his spirit willingly by himself. No man has that kind of power. No one has the power to raise it again having been dead for three days. When they came to the hewn tomb early on the first day of the week, they found the stone rolled away and an

empty grave. The angel said, *"You are looking for Jesus of Nazareth; he is not here; he is risen."* While the seal was broken at the tomb because of His resurrection, there is a seal that will forever be closed, assuring resurrection power after death. *O death, where is thy sting? O grave, where is thy victory? Thanks be unto God which gives us the victory through our Lord Jesus Christ.* Hallelujah, what a Savior! He is the fairest of ten thousand. There is none like Him, no, not one.

Jesus showed Himself alive after His passion for 40 days. He appeared to Mary Magdalene, of whom he cast out seven demons. He appeared to the disciples through locked doors and ate with them. He appeared miraculously and walked with two on the road to Emmaus. He appeared to *"Doubting Thomas"* showing the nail prints in His hands and feet. Early one morning, He showed Himself alive to Peter. At one time he showed himself alive to over 500 people. Blessed are those who have seen and believe, as well as blessed are those who have not seen and believe. This preponderance of evidence is the most accurate proof that He is who He said He was. Nothing is more convincing or has more weight of truth.

This same Jesus has ascended back to heaven, and is found at the right hand of God making intercession for believers. He came in a body prepared for Him, in the same body that died on a cross, and even now in that same body, He is touched with the feelings of our infirmities in heaven in a glorified body. Soon and very soon, He will come in that same body to catch us up into glory. With this in hand and heart, we take this good news to the world and the region beyond.

Connect

Just suppose, "had it not been..." for this Savior!

JUST A THOUGHT...

Was e'er a gift like the Savior given? No, not one! no, not one!
Will he refuse us a home in heaven? No, not one! no not one.
Jesus knows all about our struggles, He will guide till the day is done;
There's not a friend like the lowly Jesus, No, not one! no, not one!

The Example of Grace Giving

II Corinthians 8:1-7

If you had purchased a thousand shares of Google stock at $9.67 a share in August of 2004. Today it would be worth (at market price of $500.00 a share) $4,835,000.00. That is spelled with a "m"! If you had this information then, how many would want to listen? However, when preachers talk about investing your money, suddenly people have deaf ears. *"That is all you preachers do; you keep asking for more money."* Well, that criticism comes with the territory, but that is not all we preachers do. (And if I told you of some of those things that we preachers do—you would not believe it!) However, it is certainly one of the things we do. It is part of the job, and someone must do it!

Paul writes to a church who had it all, the Corinthian church. But there was one thing lacking in their portfolio—their record of grace of giving. He points to the churches of Macedonia, poor people, living far below minimum wage, having great misfortune, and with no hope of any kind of a turnaround. Anyone could out-give these people, but few knew how they gave with grace.

Where did these churches learn how to give? They gave as being the beneficiaries of grace giving, namely the example of Christ Himself. *For ye know the grace of our Lord Jesus Christ, that, though he was rich, yet for your sakes he became poor, that ye through his poverty might be rich.* Christ became the *"unspeakable gift,"* the grace giving of God Himself to us. How more blessed are we today because of Christ coming to us? He is the benevolence of God's goodness to any person who is wretched,

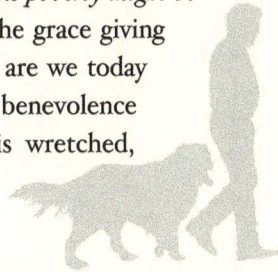

miserable, poor, blind, naked, and those who seemingly have need of nothing. Receiving Him is just simply indescribable!

Consider with me the example of grace giving by the suffering, poor Macedonians. They first gave very generously. God loves a cheerful giver, one who feels like jumping up and down hilariously when it comes to giving. Not out of deep pockets, but out of deep poverty (8:2), they emptied what they had into preachers' coffers for those hurting worse than they—grace giving. They held nothing back.

They gave voluntarily too. Out of their hearts flowed a free will love offering. You can give without loving, but you can not love without giving. *Freely you have received, freely give.* They did this not grudgingly, but freely of their own free will.

Enthusiastically! Remember that $9.67 of Google stock! These Macedonians, you got to *love 'em* and till you do grace giving, you will never get excited *like 'em!* They did not wait for someone else to pass the plate; they passed the plate and could not wait to do it. They gave with haste, urgently giving to the fellowship of ministering and to the necessity of the saints. Indeed an unspeakable gift!

Before we leave off with this, what about their selfless response? Their needs, their desires, their retirement suddenly became secondary.

—Connect—

They first gave themselves to the Lord and...being in the will of God,
they gave to men of God (8:5) for the work of the ministry.

J U S T A T H O U G H T...
This is the Father's business; take care of it, and
He will take care of your business!

Neither Could They Blush

Jeremiah 8:12

Were they ashamed when they had committed abomination? nay, they were not at all ashamed, neither could they blush: therefore shall they fall among them that fall: in the time of their visitation they shall be cast down, saith the LORD.

We have judges in Massachusetts giving full sanctions of marital rights to homosexuals and lesbians as to heterosexuals. Ninety million people saw the "heros" of the MTV world brazenly exposing nudity without shame. The seeds of Sodom and Gomorrah are springing up and growing like wildfire. We have a generation who no longer knows how to blush or be ashamed of the wickedness spewing from their hearts. Sodomy laws have become a norm and are flourishing before our eyes.

We today are encouraging drunks to be drunks as long as there is a sober driver to take them home. We are informing our kids how to engage in safe sex rather than waiting for sacred sex.

President Bush said from his State of the Union address that he is deeply troubled over the family being redefined. He told us he supports a marriage made up of one man and one woman. And I said *"Amen"* to that. God, give us more preachers who will address these issues like our beloved President.

The Bible tells us to *"hold the traditions which you have been taught"* (II Thess. 2:15). The marriage bed alone is honorable and sacred between a husband and a wife...period! *Whoremongers and adulterers will God judge.* God protected sex within the boundaries of a monogamous marriage. Maintaining this tradition will help keep the lid on this black box.

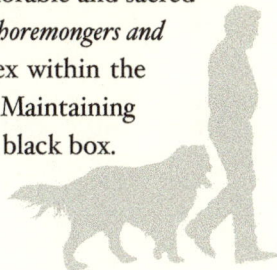

We have aborted a generation of taxpayers by murdering babies in the womb. And we wonder why every state in the union is behind on their budgets. The tradition of life and the pursuit of happiness has been shattered in the lives of some 40 million infants since 1973. Thank you, Supreme Court Justices. Their blood be upon our judges and their children.

God has not changed His mind on the first chapter of Romans. His wrath is holy, just, and is due. He will not be mocked or ridiculed. Yet, His blood can cover the most vile sins and His love is infinite. This nation must repent, turn from our wicked ways, and restore the traditions which we have been taught.

— *Connect* —

Do you think God will spare judgment on America for the same sin as Sodom was guilty of?

JUST A THOUGHT...

Are there not fifty righteous that can be found which will keep God's wrath from this land which I love?

Lord, What Do You
Want ME To Do?

Acts 9:6

Recently, I attended and viewed a simulcast from Rick Warren on the subject: *What on earth am I here for?* A powerful message that was not new from Rick's heart, but a powerful message very true from *God's heart.* He addressed the principles which God has for all people who will accept His Son Jesus Christ as their personal Savior and will follow Him in a life of obedience. Rev. Warren wrote a book about it, *The Purpose Driven Life,* a book that has sold over 30 million copies! Go get a copy.

It is not difficult to see what God is doing in the lives of others. Their lives in the service of God are as it were an open book written in the sky. But ask yourself this question: "Lord, what do you want ME to do?" There has been no other greater conversion than the apostle Paul on the Damascus Road. He was stricken blind to the ground by the power of God as he heard God's voice spoken only to him. As he fell trembling to the earth, he asked the question which we all should ask, *"Lord, what will you have ME to do?"* No matter how far away you are, He can hear you.

Do know what God wants you to do? Is there an overwhelming assurance in your soul that you are walking the chartered path which only God planned for you? And are you enjoying the services you are rendering unto Him? If so, then God bless you. There can be no greater treasure found in this world than this. You can experience

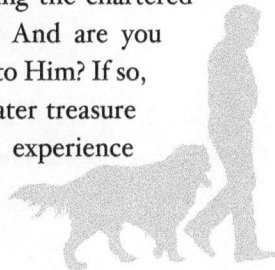

not only being saved from hell, but to understand God's will in the abundance of the Christian life. There is no greater question you can ask in this world than, *"Lord, what do you want ME to do?"* Ask Him right now; I double-dog dare you; and listen for that still quiet voice as He speaks clearly to you.

God's way in knowing what work He has for you is just simply beginning to follow the path in which you are traveling. The headlights on your truck can only lighten the path as you place it in gear and proceed ahead. God said to Saul (who became Paul), *"Arise and go into the city, and it will be told thee what thou must do."* God guides people to guide people. *"How can I except some man guide me?"* God used someone to tell me about His Son and guided me in accepting Him. As God used others to tell you about Him, He now will use you to tell others about Him. Listen, Paul went into the very city, not to see lives shattered but to see lives saved.

The will of God for you and me is not hard to understand. It is as though He has written it in large bold letters just for you and me personally. Here is how to do it. Study the Bible which was written for you and it will tell you where God is working. Sign up for a job there. As you proceed to follow, you will sense the Holy Spirit's leading. This lighted path will come to a place that has been designed specifically for you. You will know it beyond any shadow of a doubt.

Connect

You will never understand what on earth you are here for until you have fallen to the earth trembling before Him. The question then will not be, "What is the will of God, but where is the will of God?" The will of God is big; you can't miss it. Go for it.

JUST A THOUGHT...
Once you have placed your hands to this plough, do not look back, and keep going straight ahead. The path ends at His feet.

"Let Not Your Heart Be Troubled"

John 14:1-6

I'm glad our President is from the great state of Texas, and I'm glad that Texas is part of the greatest country in the world, the United States of America. Patriotism was seen at its best when President George Bush landed on the USS Abraham Lincoln Warship, supporting our troops and speaking to the nation.

Our President spoke to the world, when he said, *"We have fought for the cause of liberty, and for the peace of the world."* He went on to say, *"Our nation is more secure, the tyrant has fallen, and Iraq is free."*

As he spoke to the generation of our military, he said, *"You have taken up the highest calling of history. You are defending your country, and protecting the innocent from harm. Wherever you go, you carry a message of hope—a message that is ancient, and ever new. In the words of Isaiah the prophet: 'To the captives, Come out,—and to those in darkness, Be free.'"*

It seemed to me, there was no better place for the Commander in Chief to bring a message of hope in the midst of a storm than when he spoke from the stern of the Abraham Lincoln Warship.

Jesus Christ is our Commander in Chief. He comes to us with a message of great hope. We do not need to fear him who has power to kill the body. While in this world there is trouble on all sides, but we are not in distress...*persecuted, but not forsaken; cast down, but not destroyed* (2 Cor. 4:8,9).

We are not troubled when we do the right thing.

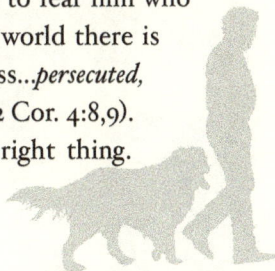

There is a peace that passes all understanding that keeps us chartered on the right course. There will be some casualties along the way, but we are not troubled or afraid of terrorism (I Pet. 3:14).

We are not troubled when the *beginning of sorrows* or end of time approaches. Whether it's wars, scares, or liars, we believe *greater is he that is in us, than he or that which is in the world.* Bloodshed, major epidemics, catastrophes, or deceivers of the highest order will not alter our course.

We are not troubled when facing our greatest enemy—death. There is a time to die, and it's appointed unto all men once to die. We are of the host who not only believe in God, we believe in Jesus Christ (John 14:1-6). As He dropped His head on a bloody chest and gave up the ghost, He, like we someday will, commended His spirit into the hands of God.

As our President said to the shipmen aboard the Abraham Lincoln, *"You want nothing more than to return home...tonight your direction is homeward bound, so likewise, our Lord says to us, 'Do not let your hearts trouble you...I will come again, and receive you unto myself; that where I am, there you may be also.'"*

— *Connect* —

Fight the good fight of faith, keep the faith, and finish your course till your battles are over in this life.

JUST A THOUGHT...
When the Commander in Chief is on board, there is confidence.

Jesus and the Woman
at the Well

John 4

The earmark of Jesus' ministry was *to seek and to save that which was lost* (Luke 19:10). He came for whosoever wheresoever. He spoke to a religious man named Nicodemus and said to him, *"Unless you are born again, you will not see or enter heaven."* He spoke to Zacchaeus, a rich man, and said to him, *"Come down; for today I must abide at your house.* In our text He speaks to a no-name rebellious woman. She was an outcast to society living in an adulterous relationship. He said to her, *"Whosoever drinks of the water that I shall give him shall never thirst: but the water that I shall give him shall be in him a well of water springing up into everlasting life."* She said, *"Sir, give me of this water."*

The story of Jesus and the woman at the well is one of the most remarkable and remembered stories of the Bible. The reader is left with principles and practices, which if properly observed and learned, he will become like Jesus, seeking the lost. There is no greater joy in the life of a Christian than to see those who are lost in sin come to Christ—none!

Jesus hates the sin but loves the sinner. No matter what heinous sin is committed, Jesus can reach them with so great salvation. You may be guilty of adultery as this woman, or guilty of murder like a Michael Shiavo, a Judge George Greer, an Attorney George Felos, or even a judiciary court and still be a recipient of the mercy of Christ.

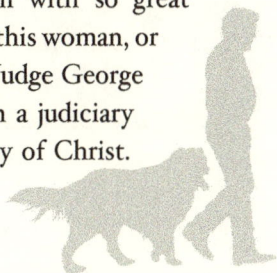

Though your sins are as scarlet or red as crimson, they can be washed in His blood and become as white as snow.

A conviction to see people saved is the driving force in being a soul-winner. Jesus made a have-to journey to see a despised woman among the Samaritans, who was a disgusted human in the eyes of man. Receiving that living water from Him, she became a believer in Christ and became a soul-winner to all she knew. Is there not a cause to go wherever to reach whosoever? Sinners won't come to you; they are dead, blind, and lost. You must go and find them.

She came for a bucket of water and left with a well of everlasting water springing up in her soul. Jesus, being God in the flesh, exposed her sin and she confessed it. She turned to God from a life of wickedness to a life of worship. She made confession of her sin and believed on Him because of His Word. Jesus sees you and me not as what we are, but what we can be. There is nothing better that can happen to any person, than for that person to confess his sin and be changed—nothing!

Her conversion piped a spiritual water supply to her world. Her story was the same story in the lives of others. What Jesus said to her was the same as what He would have said to the men in her life. Her conversion made her the mouthpiece for Christ. Many of the Samaritans believed on Him because of her testimony. Your story can become their story—go tell them what He has said to you.

— *Connect* —

If you have drunk water from this everlasting well, water that will quench definite thirst, then give a cup of this water to someone, like someone gave to you.

JUST A THOUGHT...
Some are lost; go find them, and then lead them so they can lead others.

Your Work and Labor of Love
Hebrews 6:10

For God is not unrighteous to forget your work and labor of love, which ye have showed toward his name, in that ye have ministered to the saints, and do minister.

Child of God, never, never, never minimize your work and never, never, never underestimate the power of God in your life. *Little is much when God is in it.* God used a boy's sling to bring down a giant of a man, He used a boy's lunch to feed the thousands, and He can use the fervent prayer of a (one) righteous man to avail much. If God calls you to it, He will use you in it.

Millions of people from shore to shore are thinking their help to the thousands who are homeless and heartless from the tsunami aftermath in Indonesia would be like a...*"drop of water in the ocean!"* Yet when some 200 million people are *"doing the Lord's work,"* it will flood the land in an overflow of love, prayer, and provisions. *Your work and labor of love* can help and will help.

God is calling laborers for a harvest. He gives opportunities to His children to participate in His work—a work that is eternal. His rewards will be great in that day when we stand before Him. He will remember you and will say, *"Well done, good and faithful servant; you have been faithful over a few things, I will make you ruler over many things: enter thou into the joy of thy Lord."* He will be no debtor to any man, and He will forget no man for the work that goes on in His name for the kingdom. No man will lose his reward, even when giving only a cup of cold water in the name of the Lord. There will be *payday someday* for kingdom workers!

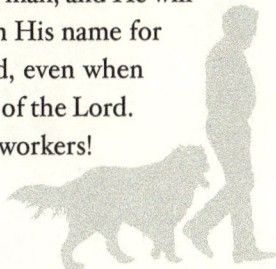

Doing the Lord's work is a way of life for the child of God. While he may get tired being in the work, he will never get tired of the work. He loves his job and loves doing it. He does it as a servant, not as a lord. He has no merit or retirement, only to please his master. When the Lord says, *"Who will go for us?"* he is the first one in line, who will say, *"Here am I, send me."* This worker is motivated only by love and will never stop doing what he loves to do. He is like the ever-ready bunny, he just keeps going. His work is a ministry, be it with a hammer, a cleaning cloth, as a CEO, or just as a prayer warrior. He has been equipped and is qualified to do His work.

A labor of love is seen as being gracious and kind. The love behind kind actions prompts the receiving of the gift without guilt or embarrassment. It becomes noble and noteworthy—*"I will never forget you and your work."* The sinner which you have just led to Christ will never forget God, or you for being used of God.

Participants in the work see it big when it is once in a lifetime to act. Like the woman with the alabaster box of costly ointment, giving extravagantly. They do what they have been called to do; they do it because it will have heaven's blessing on it and God's stamp of approval. In doing so, they are in a state of worship as being guided by the Holy Spirit. And...they will always tell others about JESUS!

— Connect

We come and receive without money or price; go and do likewise.

J ust a thought...
Others see your work that goes on before;
God sees what is behind your work.

Living in a Sinful World
John 17:11-16

This world is a system by which people are governed by science, politics, religion, and philosophy. It is also governed by lust, which is primarily against God and His Word. It is a world full of murderers, whoremongers, thieves, liars, sin, deceivers, drugs, immorality, idolaters, and the devil. It is a world that God loved so much that He sent His only begotten Son to come to live and to die in the hands of evil men.

Christ saves us and then leaves us in this sinful world. Jesus prayed, *"I pray not that you take them out of the world, but that you should keep them from evil. They are not of the world, even as I am not of the world. Sanctify them through thy truth: thy word is truth"* (John 17:15-17).

Gypsy Smith once said, *"If you are in with this world, then you are out with God."* Hogs live quietly and comfortably with the dirt, slop, and filth. Goats will enjoy everything or anything they can eat. Dogs will always return to their vomit. Sheep, however, will fall into the slime pits, but they are not at ease there. Vance Havner said, *"We feel at home where we belong."*

How then should we live in a sinful world?

Live like Jesus did while He was here. He glorified the Father in His death on a cross (1). In this supreme test of life and before His death, Jesus said, *"Father, forgive them, for they know not what they do."* If you do not know how to love the worst of men, then you do not know not how to live in a sinful world.

Work the work which God has given you to do (4). Jesus said, *"I have finished the work which you gave me."*

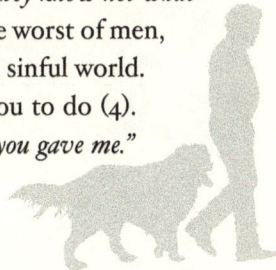

Mom used to tell me, *"Idleness is the devil's workshop."* Sumner Wemp says, *"You can quit when the devil does."* Paul says, *"I have fought a good fight, kept the faith, and finished my course."*

Pray while you are in this sinful world. Jesus did (9): *"I pray for them."* If He needed to pray, how much more do you and I? When Job prayed for his three miserable friends, God turned his captivity and gave him a double portion.

Read the Word of God (14), love not this world (14), and get a mission statement for life—*"as you have sent me, so I have sent them into this world"* (18). We are not to be isolationists, but rather bridge-builders, going over to where they are, that we might win them for Jesus. Telling others about God, heaven, hell, Satan, Jesus, glorifying the Father, and how they can live a Holy Spirit-filled life.

— Connect —

His mission becomes our mission and the very reason why God left us in this sinful world.

JUST A THOUGHT...
What has God called you to do in this sinful world?
If you are not dead, you should be working!

Our Lord's Last Words

Matthew 28:18-20

The church is the most powerful, influential, and wonderful of all organizations. She has been battered, beaten, and bruised, yet she remains to be a blessing to all who cross her paths—and her doors are open today to some 7 billion persons who live on this earth.

The work which God is doing today is through the local church. In America, there are more than 200,000 local, evangelical churches who still believe the Gospel message of the Lord Jesus Christ. Churches who preach *the blood, the book, and the blessed hope.* And from a land which has only 6% of the total world's population, America is sending out 96% of all the missionaries known in the world.

Our Lord's Last Words has been coined as the *Great Commission: And Jesus came and spake unto them, saying, All power is given unto me in heaven and in earth. Go ye therefore, and teach all nations, baptizing them in the name of the Father, and of the Son, and of the Holy Ghost: Teaching them to observe all things which I have commanded you: and lo, I am with you always, even unto the end of the world. Amen* (Matt. 28:18-20).

All power is given unto the Lord, power which He has given unto the church. There is no other means by which this mammoth work can persevere than through His power. The message is simple: the death, burial, and the resurrection. When believed, believers are immersed in water in the name of the Father, the Son, and the Holy Ghost. The method has never been changed: *"Go ye..."* People reaching people, a one-on-one method.

His last words were immutable. Words which have never been improved on and have never been altered. He spoke with all authority and enabled those who would hear to go with all authority. *They went everywhere preaching the gospel...* Words which have never been rescinded—thus the reason that after 2,000 years we are still going!

His last words were imperative. *Go ye into all the world...* These words came from one whom they would die for. They came as the last words ever to be remembered from Him. They would receive these words as soldiers marching as unto war. There was no time for retirement, not one of them resigned, they would have no regrets, and they died having no remorse. These last words were clear, brief, comprehensive, and commanding, coming from the one who would always be with them. Not one of them who heard these words ever failed in going. Neither should any of us!

His words were imminent. *"Go ye therefore..."* as if He were saying go ye now. They became servants of the Father's business which demanded haste. What they did, they did quickly. They believed their mission, should they accept it, was to reach their world in their lifetime. Acts 17 states that these turned the world upside down with the Gospel. All people are within one heartbeat of eternity; they are as Jude tells us, in the fire, and we without hesitation must reach them. Just do it; it's our duty!

— *Connect* —

The method had never been changed for you and me: "Go ye..."
People reaching people in a personal one-on-one encounter.

JUST A THOUGHT...
What was the last thing Jesus said to you?

The Man With
a Pitcher of Water

Mark 14:12-16

And the first day of unleavened bread, *when they killed the passover, his disciples said unto him, Where do you want us to go and prepare that you may eat the passover? And he sent out two of his disciples, and said unto them, Go ye into the city, and there a man shall meet you bearing a pitcher of water: follow him. And wherever he shall go in, say ye to the goodman of the house, The Master says, Where is the guestchamber, where I shall eat the passover with my disciples? And he will show you a large upper room furnished and made ready: there make ready for us. And his disciples went out, and came into the city, and found as he had said unto them: and they made ready the passover.*

Life is full of questions and decisions. There are decisions facing every one of us every day. We know where point *A* is, but how do we get to point *B?* At times we do not even know where point *B* is! Our loving gracious Father God has given to us many guides in life. If we are sensitive to His will, He will guide us namely by His Spirit through those who are around us. Your pastor is God's man that has come to the kingdom and in our life for such a time as this. *He is not that Light, but is sent to bear witness of that Light. That was the true Light, which lights every man that comes into the world.*

Go and you will find a man (significantly) bearing a pitcher of water. Look not for *them,* look not for *her,* but look for the *man.* As in this case of the disciples, there was no question as to whom this man would be—for

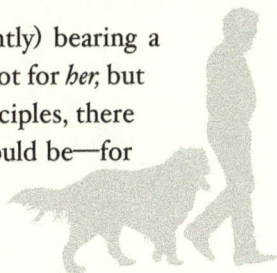

women in that day normally carried pitchers of water. There would be only one man found carrying a pitcher of water on that day. Mark him as the man that will lead you to the upper room. Go, there will be no mistake in finding this man!

When you have found this man, then follow him. Follow him as he follows Christ. Follow him as he gives clear directions from the Scriptures, follow him as to the leading of the Holy Spirit in his life, and follow him after he has spent many hours in prayer. Follow him as you would follow the man of God, follow him as your God-called pastor, and follow him in whatever the Lord's will is in your life. *He has set some in the church...pastors and teachers.* He is there for you; he will be there for you; follow him!

And his disciples went out and found as he had said to them. Neither you nor I will ever forget those who have been used in our lives to bring us to Christ or to lead us in service of our Lord.

What do we find in that upper room? We find God's only begotten Son. It is here that the Father seeks such to worship Him. We find fellowship with Him and with those who love Him. We find ourselves growing into His image as we draw near to Him. We find ourselves being shaped for ministry. And then we find our mission to evangelize the world. This handful of disciples went out and turned the world upside down. All of this and heaven too, all because of a man of God who crossed their path carrying a pitcher of water. Follow HIM!

— *Connect* —

Were it not for the people we have met or the books we have read, we can only imagine where we would be.

JUST A THOUGHT...
 Thank God for the man of God He sent our way!

"The Last Lap"
Psalm 39:4-12

LORD, make me to know mine end, and the measure of my days, what it is; that I may know how frail I am.

Dale Earnhardt, at 49 years of age and a 7-time Winston Cup NASCAR champion, was killed on the *Last Lap* of the Daytona 500, Sunday, February 18, 2001. His famous Chevrolet Black Monte Carlo # 3 crashed into the concrete wall at a high rate of speed. A NASCAR driver for more than 20 years!

His death has been compared to those of Jimmy Dean and Princess Diana. He leaves behind a grieving wife (Teresa), a family, and millions of fans across America. His time on earth was far too short for many.

James 4:14 says, *"You do not know what will happen tomorrow. For what is your life? It is even a vapor that appears for a little time and then vanishes away."* Life as we know it at its longest is relatively short. I can say of the past 63 years—life has been very short. Life can come to a sudden stop with little preparation and leaving so many things left to be done. I'm sure Dale Earnhardt was planning on finishing the Daytona 500 race at Rockingham, NC, and all the other races left in this brand-new NASCAR season. That Sunday was his last race and his *last lap!*

We all are victims in life's race. We all alike will die, but we all will not die alike. *It rains on the just as well as on the unjust.* Life and death is no respecter of persons. Death is the last appointment in living. If we are not prepared to die, then we are not prepared to live. We must be ready to die; we do not know the hour of our death. Sin is the

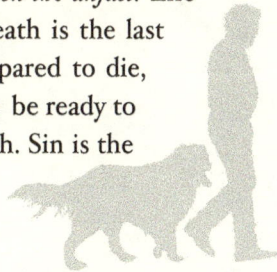

number one killer of the human race, which will take all of us out on our *last lap* in life.

Take your Bible and read some of the verses like: Heb. 9:27, Psa. 89:47, Phil. 1:21, and John 14:6. Listen to these verses closely and live by them. Stevie Waltrip gave a verse, Prov. 18:10, to Dale Earnhardt on Sunday's race. He stuck it on his dashboard: *"The name of the Lord is a strong tower; the righteous man rushes into it and finds refuge!"*

Victory lane is just ahead for all of us! I Cor. 15:57—*"Thanks be to God which gives us the victory."* Rev. Max Helton, the founder of the Motor Racing Outreach, prayed for Dale before he began the Daytona 500. He also prayed for the family and with the family at the hospital. Dale Earnhardt was not only a great family man, a fine businessman, a NASCAR driver, but like Sunday's race, he was a companion of a great NASCAR driver...Michael Waltrip. But the champion Dale followed in life was Jesus Christ. On his last day, in his last race, on his *last lap*—he entered the victory lane...in heaven!

— *Connect* —

Get Bible verses like these and tape them
to your dashboard for your last lap.

J U S T   A   T H O U G H T ...
Life today promises no tomorrows!

Sleeping Through a Storm

Mark 4:37

And there arose a great storm of wind, and
the waves beat into the ship, so that it was now full.

Jesus said to His disciples, *"Let's pass over to the other side."* He was
sending these right into a *"killer storm."* Not only His disciples, but
others who were in other little ships too. When they set sail, there
seemingly was no awareness of any danger, all was calm, destiny straight
ahead, and Jesus on board. No problem!

Suddenly there was a great storm and waves, a *"perfect storm."* There
was a great fear, and they thought they possibly would not make it
to the other side. Now where was Jesus when they needed Him? The
Bible says He was found sleeping on a pillow. Had they not awakened
Him, Jesus would have slept right through the storm. (Right now, get
a pillow and hold on to it; we will come back to it in a moment.) He
spoke to the wind as if He spoke to the devil, in a voice of authority
and command, for it was indeed a killer storm. *"Stop it,"* and the great
storm became a great calm. What manner of man can say to the wind
to cease and it obeys Him?

As long as Jesus is on board, there will be nothing to keep us from
getting to the other side. Storms will come and go, and they make great
stories to tell to our grandchildren. If we never knew of them, how
then would we ever know how Jesus could ever stop them?
So, say to Satan, "Bring it on; give me your best shot. See
if you can take us out."

You can sleep through any storm if you know who
you are. You are God's child and He will not let you

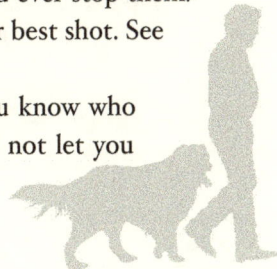

sink. You can sleep through any storm if you know where you are going. You are going to heaven, and God has given you His Word on that! You can sleep through any storm if you know that Jesus is in your life. He said, *"I will never leave you nor forsake you."* Just as the three Hebrew children were in the midst of the fire, there was found a fourth man. It was Jesus—the Son of God. As He was with them, He will be with you.

You can sleep through a storm if you know where Jesus is in your life. You can sleep through a storm if you know that Jesus can stop any storm. You can sleep through a storm knowing Jesus has never lost any in a storm. You can sleep through any storm knowing you will be stronger having gone through storms. You can sleep through a storm knowing you have slept through many other storms in your life, and this one will soon pass as well. You can sleep through any storm knowing God's will for your life. You can sleep through a storm knowing it is Jesus who is sending you into it.

Now concerning that pillow you are holding, the only time the word *pillow* is mentioned in the New Testament is in this text. Jesus used a pillow to sleep during a storm and you can too. It is not a pillow that will carry you through, but the one sleeping on that pillow. The Bible says, *"...as he is, so are we in this world."* Now lay your head down as He did and get some rest.

— *Connect* —

Get a pillow, and use it when the next storm comes in your life.
You will make it!

JUST A THOUGHT...
Do you have any stories to tell about storms?
If so, you have lived through them.

The Lord's Supper

I Corinthians 11:26

For as often as ye eat this bread, and drink this
cup, ye do shew the Lord's death till he come.

The Bible says on the night when our Lord was betrayed, He observed the fellowship with His disciples by taking bread and drinking from a cup. (See I Cor. 11:23-30). The Lord's Supper—there is no better time for worship and no better time to feel close to Him. So close that if it were possible, we like John would lay our head on the bosom of Christ!

It is regarded as one of the two ordinances of the church, the other being baptism. It is only for believers who have come to Christ for the forgiveness of sin through the shedding of His blood and the sacrifice of His body on the cross. When the family of God comes together at His table, the bread speaks of His body and the contents of the cup speaks of His blood. While many will differ and even cause division over this church doctrine, the Lord's Supper is a time of reflecting of the sufferings on the cross where our *Lord tasted death for every person.* He has called the church together to remember what it took for salvation to be real to everyone who believes the Gospel.

The Lord's Supper is a time of giving thanks. *"Thank you, Lord, for saving my soul; thank you, Lord, for making me whole..."* a great song of the church. Far too many of us at times have forgotten the Rock from which we were hewn. We become so busy about the work of the Lord that we forget the Lord of the work. *"We know the work of the Lord, but we do not know the Lord of the work"* (Jeanie Hartley). If it were not for Christ's

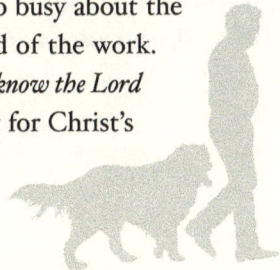

death on the cross, we all would be most miserable and hopelessly lost. *"When he had given thanks...."* Thank Him, not some preacher!

The schedule of the Lord's Supper is not an issue, but observing it is. It is not when you do it, but how you will do it. Some take it every Sunday, some the first of the month, some as in the days of the disciples took it every day, while others will observe it occasionally. We should participate in it *"often,"* never missing an opportunity with repetition and with readiness to share with others.

The Lord's Supper is His supper being observed in His church. It is His table and He calls for all His family to come. It is a time for brothers and sisters to come around His table with Him. If you have been washed in His blood and cleansed from your sins, you now can come to His table. *Let a man examine himself.* This is not for any church council to control, only a believer can do this. Jesus is giving us a personal invitation to come and be near Him.

The Lord's Supper is a serious undertaking. Some come *"unworthily,"* with a "flippant attitude." It's only a meal, big deal! This manner will bring either chastisement or judgment. When the sufferings and the brutal death of our Lord on a cruel cross does not move us, it will move the discipling hand of God against believers now and against the unsaved in eternity.

—Connect—

*In His presence and remembering what it took for you to be there...
there is nothing that captures your attention for the moment
like the Lord's Supper!*

JUST A THOUGHT...
*Unless you eat of this bread and drink of this cup,
you have no life in you.*

What a Friend We Have in Jesus

Hebrews 13:8

Jesus Christ the same yesterday, and to day, and for ever.

Someone has said, "One friend is better than a thousand acquaintances." Another has said, "When you die, one can only name real true friends on one hand." Yet another has said, "A true friend is one who walks in when others walk away from you." There are those times in one's life when a real friend is more close than blood relatives. Such is true with Jesus—*"He is a friend that sticks closer than a brother!"*

Friendship which is knitted together with spiritual intimacy is a level beyond any natural relationship. *"Jonathan loved David as his own soul."* Their love for each other was rare, unique, and special. They knew all they could about each other, and yet their friendship never wavered once!

Jesus is our friend, one who will never walk away from us anytime or anywhere. He is even a friend to sinners and publicans, the worst kind of people. His love for the world is to the end of the world. Many things He is to all of us, yet being a friend is one which will draw all of us to Him.

He is my oldest friend. Nothing will ever equate like having an old friend. One who will always be there to hear of your burdens and one who will never change his opinion about you. Jesus has been my friend since the day of my birth. He knows all about me, and remains the same toward me!

He is my dearest friend. I can go to Him with anything! He understands my thoughts which are

far off, He is patient and longsuffering with me, and one that can love me when I'm unlovable. If only there were words to describe this relationship which I have in Jesus.

He is my closest, most honest, and most generous friend. He has promised to remain the same, tell me what I need to hear, and always be there to meet my needs. There will never be a friend that will ever be as close to you, or will tell you where you have gone wrong, or so gracious to give you even Himself. What a friend we have in Him!

There is one thing which we all do with our friends, that is to introduce our friends to others. Remember, when you are talking to a friend, He is in the midst of the company. Introduce Him and let Him speak!

— *Connect* —

Won't you find people whom you can tell about Jesus?
It will be the best thing you could ever do for them.
It will change their lives and their eternal address forever!

JUST A THOUGHT...
The greatest thing you can do for your friend
is to introduce him to Christ.

The Twenty-Third Psalm
Psalm 23

The LORD is my shepherd; I shall not want. He maketh me to lie down in green pastures: he leadeth me beside the still waters. He restoreth my soul: he leadeth me in the paths of righteousness for his name's sake. Yea, though I walk through the valley of the shadow of death, I will fear no evil: for thou art with me; thy rod and thy staff they comfort me. Thou preparest a table before me in the presence of mine enemies: thou anointest my head with oil; my cup runneth over. Surely goodness and mercy shall follow me all the days of my life: and I will dwell in the house of the LORD forever.

The Twenty-Third Psalm is the best loved and most read chapter in all the Bible. It is by far the most read chapter every day in the war-torn country of Iraq. There is comfort and joy every time we read or hear this chapter read. We never tire in its words, in its content, or its illustrations. It is as filling and refreshing after many years as it was upon the first time of its presentation to us. Most often we find this passage on some program during a funeral service—and how timely and fitting. There is no better time to comfort those who are hurting with the Word of God than at this time. Somehow it unlocks the windows of heaven which allows the sunlight of God's love to fill a very vacant and dark room that has consumed us.

The Lord is my shepherd... If that were all we had in this brief chapter, it would be enough. Volumes of books could fill libraries alone on each of those words. And because He is my present and forever Shepherd, there is nothing in this world that could ever compare to the satisfying

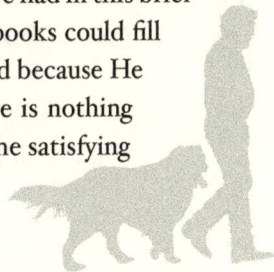

of the soul. If sheep could talk, they no doubt would confirm: *He is the fairest of the valley, the bright and morning star!*

Green pastures and still waters are all around me, in me, and under me, and one day waiting for me. In Him I have rest for the soul as I make my journey through life. The provisions for my travel are found everywhere.

He restores my soul. The restoration of my soul is a daily need. As sheep it is so easy and tempting to stray from the fold, and all we like sheep have been led astray by others from the fold. He is ever there to seek, find, and bring us home by showing the correct paths to follow, the paths of righteousness.

Yea, though I walk through the valley of the shadow of death every waking moment of our lives, yet we *fear no evil.* Why? *For thou art with me.* There is no death in His presence, only life. There is no evil in Him, only right, goodness, and truth. Let the lion and the bear come, the rod and staff will give defense and direction in life. As He was with Joseph, Daniel, Jeremiah, and a host of others, even so He will be with me. Hallelujah, what a Shepherd!

And I will dwell in the house of the Lord forever. This road believers are traveling will lead us all the way to the Father's house, where we will dwell with Him forever. Goodness and mercy have been with me all my life: *Thou preparest a table before me in the presence of mine enemies.* The Holy Spirit is my companion, and my cup is full. All of that and heaven too because the Good Shepherd gave His life for His sheep!

—Connect—

The Lord is my Shepherd...what more do I want?

JUST A THOUGHT...
The Twenty-Third Psalm, what else shall we say?

John Three Sixteen
John 3:16

The church's pastor slowly stood up, walked over to the pulpit, and, before he gave his sermon for the evening, briefly introduced a guest minister who was in the service that evening. In the introduction, the pastor told the congregation that the guest minister was one of his dearest childhood friends and that he wanted him to have a few moments to greet the church and share whatever he felt would be appropriate for the service. With that, an elderly man stepped up to the pulpit and began to speak. He began with this story: A father, his son, and a friend of his son were sailing off the Pacific Coast when a fast-approaching storm blocked any attempt to get back to the shore. The waves were so high that even though the father was an experienced sailor, he could not keep the boat upright, and the three were swept into the ocean as the boat capsized.

The old man hesitated for a moment, making eye contact with two teenagers who for the first time since the service began were looking somewhat interested in his story. The aged minister continued with his story. Grabbing a rescue line, the father had to make the most excruciating decision of his life: To which boy would he throw the other end of the lifeline? He only had seconds to make the decision. The father knew that his son was a Christian, and he also knew that his son's friend was not.

The agony of his decision could not be matched by the torrent of waves. As the father yelled out, "I love you, son!" he threw out the lifeline to his son's friend.

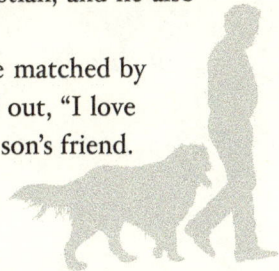

By the time the father had pulled the friend back to the capsized boat, his son had disappeared beneath the raging swells into the black of night. His body was never recovered.

By this time, the two teenagers were sitting up straight in the pew, anxiously waiting for the next words to come out of the old man.

He continued: The father knew his son would step into eternity with Jesus, and he could not bear the thought of his son's friend stepping into an eternity without Jesus. Therefore, he sacrificed his son to save the son's friend. The old preacher went on to say, "How great is the love of God that He should do the same for us. Our heavenly Father sacrificed His only begotten Son that we could be saved. I urge you to accept His offer to rescue you and take ahold of the lifeline He is throwing out to you in this service."

With that, the old man turned and sat back down in his chair as silence filled the room. The pastor again walked slowly to the pulpit and delivered a brief sermon with an invitation at the end. However, no one responded to the appeal. Within minutes after the service ended, the two teenagers were at the old man's side.

"That was a nice story," politely stated one of the boys, "but I don't think it was very realistic for a father to give up his only son's life in hopes that the other boy would become a Christian." "Well, you've got a point there," the old man replied, glancing down at his worn Bible. A big smile broadened his narrow face as he once again looked up at the boys and said, "It sure isn't very realistic, is it? But I'm standing here today to tell you that this story gives me a glimpse of what it must have been like for God to give up His Son for me. You see I was that father and your pastor was my son's friend."

Connect

If you so feel led, tell this story to your friends.

JUST A THOUGHT...
Oh, what unimaginable love!

The Message of
the Apostle Paul
I Timothy 2:4-6

Who will have all men to be saved, and to come unto the knowledge of the truth. For there is one God, and one mediator between God and men, the man Christ Jesus; Who gave himself a ransom for all, to be testified in due time.

Jesus said, *"The Son of man came...to give his life a ransom for many."* Paul said, *"Who (Jesus) gave his life a ransom for all."* This is the trust of the Gospel from the one who is the Gospel to the one who will be faithful preaching the Gospel. It is the message for all men so anyone can come to the knowledge of the truth so that anyone can be saved. Saved how? The message is one: *One mediator between God and men, the man Christ Jesus.*

Jesus Christ, *"who...took upon himself the form of a servant, and was made in the likeness of men: And being found in fashion as a man, he humbled himself, and became obedient unto death, even the death of the cross"* (Phil 2:7,8). In this He became the mediator, the arbitrator between God and all prisoners who sit on death row, who alone can bring peace through Him. Note that there is "one mediator," Jesus Christ. Only Christ alone can reconcile anyone who is guilty of sin and restore that which is lost. Christ's blood alone is the only price that can satisfy the demands of God for the cost of sin. Jesus Christ Himself is that all-redeeming sacrifice, once and for all.

This was the message of Jesus Christ, the message of the apostle Paul, and it must be the message of every Gospel preacher who will tell the truth about the truth.

Who will have all men to be saved. God loves all people. He is not a respecter of any, and His will is that all men will be saved. He is not willing that any perish, but that all will come to Him. Any that will come will not be cast out. It is therefore not that any can not come; it is because they will not come. Jesus said, as He wept over the city of Jerusalem with love, that He would bring men to Himself as a hen would her brood...*but ye would not.* All men: men who are morally delinquent, spiritually bankrupt, and those who are scripturally lost. All have sinned and come short, but all men can come to Christ. That was Paul's message and this is my message too.

To come to the knowledge of the truth. Coming to the place where there is absolutely no question, no doubt, and no confusion as to the reality of Jesus Christ. Jesus is the Christ, the Christos, the Messiah. He is all that the Old Testament said about Him who came and was testified by those who saw Him in due time. He was God's incarnate Son in human flesh, born of a virgin, lived a pure and sinless life, and died vicariously on a sinner's cross. He was buried in a borrowed tomb and got up on the third day.

Paul echos the message of the Gospel. *I speak the truth in Christ, and lie not* (I Tim. 2:7). He says it like it is, in season and out of season. He says it before those who would make him a god as well as to the one who would stone him. He did not falsify or water down the message—he presented it in full strength, even if it meant his own death. Christ is that man for all men; there are no exceptions...period!

— *Connect* ————————————

What is the content of your message according to the Gospel truth?

J UST A THOUGHT...
  If there is not only one message, how many are there?

The Valley of the
Shadow of Death
Psalm 23:4

"*Yea*"—with certainty, we are all in the valley of death. A valley that is always deep, dark, and dangerous. From the moment of conception, lurking all around us, is the shadow of life's greatest enemy, death!

Can the Shepherd still protect His sheep from the ripping paw of the bear or the bone-crushing jaw of the lion? Do we really believe if God has delivered us from the power of these in the past, that He can still do it? If so, then why didn't God protect the seven who lost their lives on the Columbia Space Shuttle on Feb. 1, 2003? Why didn't God protect us from the thugs of terrorism on Sept. 11, 2001? And at this time, why have we lost over 2,600 soldiers in the Iraq War?

Satan is the author of death. He has come *to steal, kill, and destroy*. As a roaring lion, *he is seeking whom he may devour.* He is a liar, a deceiver, and a murderer. There is not one sheep that he does not want. This serial killer will not stop killing until he is hurled into the lake of fire. He is the ultimate terrorist!

One thing is clear, no matter how deep this valley may be, or how long it may be, the Shepherd of the sheep will get us *through* it. While we may be in the valley of death, we will go through it. If by reason we take our last step and breathe our last breath in this valley, the next step and breath will be on the other side. However, if our last days be in the valley, we go down victorious. *O death, where is thy sting? O grave, where is thy victory?*

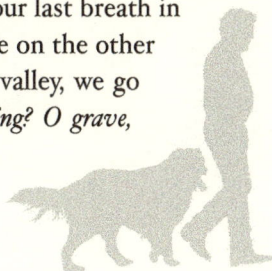

I will fear no evil, for thou art with me. This is His Word, it's a promise. He said He would be with me, would never leave me nor forsake me. In those midnight hours, I want Him with me. There is no fear to him which has power to kill the body. For an example, when they cut Paul's head off, God picked it up and put a crown on it. Jesus said, *"Father, into thy hands I commend my spirit."* The Lord is my Shepherd; His presence is always with me, even facing death.

Thy rod and thy staff they comfort me. The rod is for our defense. We can fight off the bear and the lion that would tear the flock apart. We are stewards committed to God's trust and good stewards we shall be. It is His rod given to us to use. The staff is for our direction. It goes before us, clearing the way. It is His staff given to us to use. If by chance we fail to use His gifts as we make this journey in this oftentimes lonely pathway, we may indeed suffer the casualties of life. The rod and the staff are ours given by the Shepherd for peace during our course in the valley of the shadow of death. The Lord is my Shepherd; His peace is always with me, even facing life's greatest enemy.

Connect

Take God at His Word when facing life's most supreme test, and you will be able to handle anything that comes your way.

JUST A THOUGHT...
Satan is a sheep-killing, bloodthirsty monster.

Christ Versus Belial

II Corinthians 6:15

The moment of truth comes when politicians of the political arena go head to head as voters express their hearts and heads in national elections. There is controversy, confusion, and conflict as the two candidates attack each other's ability to govern Congress, states, or even our country. We go to the polls and vote.

However, the conflict of the ages rages today with more severity of intensity as the ultimate superpowers of the universe collide in battle over the most coveted crown: namely the souls of mankind. It is the conflict of *Christ and Belial*. Make no mistake about it, there is no concord here, there can be no settlement reached to avoid a showdown, and at the end of the day there will be a crowning victory and a stunning defeat. Christ will win over this deserter, this dragon, this evil wicked one, this useless and worthless one, this devil, and this Belial. These two arch rivals are now and will be forever worlds apart. Satan is this Belial and knows he has but a short time. He is going down!

The declaration has been made, the battle lines have been drawn, and the troops have been called up. We have been summoned to the front line to press against the forces of hell. We have no fear, we will not fret, and we will not fail. We have a mandate, the Commander in Chief is our Lord, and our orders are in hand. *"Onward Christian soldiers, marching as to war...!"*

President George Bush recently said, *"Time is running out,"* and so it is. Time is running out for the church to reach the masses for Christ. The church must

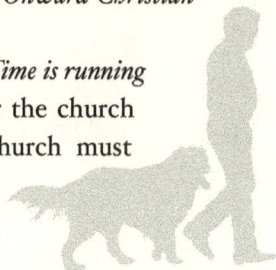

train missionaries and have them ready to go when called up (Acts 13). We must teach the Word of God, be trained with that double-edged sword, which will enable the spiritual warrior to bring down the mighty strongholds of Satan. We must pray in faith for strength and endurance. We must use our spiritual gifts, give of our time and our resources to build up a reserve of power to the second, third, and fourth ranks. And we must never, never, never quit or retreat.

Words from the Bible have encouraged us. Words like triumph, victory, and conquerors build holy faith. Heroes of the past who grace the galleries of heaven's grandstands are cheering us on. They rejoice over the souls won. Landmarks keep us walking point, such as the cross of Christ and the empty grave, keeping us on that straight and narrow path. We are not deceived, we are not discouraged, and we will not get detoured on this chartered course.

Make no mistake about it, the outcome of this debate is as if it had already happened. Christ will emerge as the victor and will reign forever as King of kings (politically) and Lord of lords (spiritually). Align yourself now with the winner of this war.

—— *Connect* ————

Keep on, child of God, Belial will concede. Keep on, child of God, until we crown Him with many crowns, the Lamb upon His throne!

JUST A THOUGHT...
   Align yourself now with the winner of this war.

What is Northside Saying to Millerburg, Ohio?

Acts 1:8

But you shall receive power after the Holy Ghost is come upon you: and you shall be witnesses unto me both in Jerusalem and in all Judea, and in Samaria, and unto the uttermost part of the earth.

This is the message from our "CEO," "Commander in Chief," the soon coming and reigning King of kings. He has been the head of the church for more than 2,000 years. Our Lord, our Master, and the Savior of the world has given the local New Testament Church its method and message to reach every soul in the entire world. *"Ye shall be witnesses unto me..."* For us who are at the Northside Baptist Church, it's in Millersburg, Ohio!

Northside Baptist Church is saying to our town in Millersburg and surrounding areas, *there is condemnation to all outside of Christ.* It makes no difference who you are, where you are, or how well you are. If you are not in Christ, you are outside of Him. All have sinned, all have transgressed against God, all are guilty before God. The message from Northside is clear—because of one man's sin, all men have sinned and are lost outside of Christ. Northside is saying there is no other way, no other truth, no other life, except through Christ and Him alone. Today, right now, there is hope, but you need to come to Christ.

Northside Baptist Church is saying to our town in Millersburg and surrounding areas—*call upon Christ.*

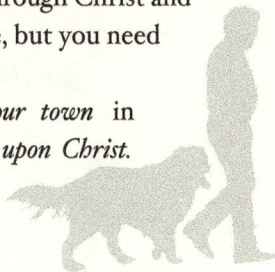

When one comes to Christ by calling on His name, there is now no condemnation to those who are found in Him. One does not have to go to Mecca, Mohammad, or even come to Millersburg. Only call upon the Lord Jesus. Feelings are not needed, finding more truth is not needed, or forsaking wicked ways are not needed—just make that call; it's a simple call in faith. *For whosoever shall call upon the name of the Lord shall be saved.* It is not what you have to know to be saved, but whom you must know. We are saying from our pulpit to our town and through some 4,500 Southern Baptist missionaries—come to Christ and call on His name. *He that heareth and believeth on me...shall not be condemned.*

Northside Baptist Church is saying to our town in Millersburg and surrounding areas, there is a *cause for Christ.* God has a will and a plan for your life after being saved. There is a reason to live and a joy unspeakable to those who walk not after the flesh, but after the Spirit. Follow the Lord in believer's baptism, join a Bible-preaching church, read the Bible, give your tithes, and go out and win someone to Christ. When there is a cause, there will be an effect. The first day of business of coming to Christ is to serve Him in the will He has for you. The purpose is to go out and make more disciples just like Jesus. *Northside* is saying, here is a church where one can grow in the knowledge and service to Christ. When standing before Him at the end of the day, hearing those words: *"Well done,"* you will be well pleased that you came, and served as a Christian!

— Connect

Northside Baptist Church is a great church with great people.
When in the area, visit and worship with us sometime.

JUST A THOUGHT...
Say, where is your church and what is your pastor's name?

The Heathen–Are They Saved?

Romans 10:9-17

For whosoever shall call upon the name
of the Lord shall be saved.

How many times have you heard the Gospel (the sufferings of Christ, His death, burial, and resurrection)? A 100 times, 500, or maybe 10,000 times you have heard that God so loved the world, that He gave His only Son to die on a cross. While it is hard to believe, there are some in this 21st century who have never heard *that he was buried, and that he rose again the third day according to the Scriptures*—not once! Not even one time!

What about those who are living today in the most remote third-world countries on earth who have never heard this good news? *How shall they call upon him in whom they have not believed?* Are these lost because they do not know the Jesus which you and I have heard and have known for so long? Would a loving God send a poor soul to a Christless hell just because they did not have an opportunity to believe?

When man sinned against God in the Garden of Eden, it made all men after him sinners in His sight. All persons are born innocently pure, but there comes a time when we sin willfully and therefore become accountable. The Bible says, *There is not one good, no not one.* Man is not a robot; he is a free moral agent, a creation of God who makes choices in life. Adam chose to sin, and sin took his life. We too chose to sin and sin is what will take our lives.

Now, for man to be saved, it will require a Savior to come and meet the holy demands of God for the payment of sin. NOTE: God did not have to be

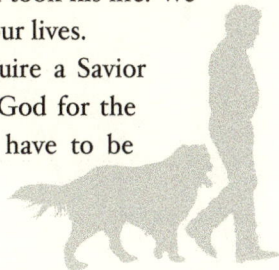

obligated to save man after He rebelled against Him. However, God loved all of us in that while we were sinners, He sent Christ to become sin for us and taste death for every man (Rom. 5:8).

The plan was cut and delivered to the world—JESUS, the Savior, who came according to the Scriptures. This is purely grace, mercy, and love to reach out to a hell-deserving, *"no-good sinner like me."*

So then what does it take to save us? Whatever it takes, it takes the same for the heathen as well wherever they are found. James Dobson (Focus on the Family) tells the story how he was saved at three years of age! It is a simple *call* upon the name of the Lord that will save you. *There is no other name given whereby we are saved*—only the name of Jesus.

Our God is a holy God, but is also fair. If any (consider the worst of men) would *call,* that person will be saved. To *call,* one must first hear. *How shall they hear without a preacher? To believe is to trust in faith—faith comes by the hearing of the word.* Salvation can only come when one *hears* and *calls* on His name.

Connect

You and I can reach the heathen with the Gospel by supporting the missionary program in our church.

JUST A THOUGHT...
> *All who are outside of Christ are lost until they are found.*

America, the Beautiful

Proverbs 14:34

Where are you, Kate Smith? Remember when she sang, "God bless America," and how it made us all proud of this land so richly blessed of God? She made us so thankful for God's goodness and His grace, and we stood in ovation as we gave Him the glory when she sang so beautifully. Oh, Kate Smith, could you not sing for the world one more time?!

America: 230 years old (1776-2006) and a land full of liberty, freedom, and opportunity. Some 300 million United States citizens can fly *"Old Glory,"* attend parades, watch the fireworks as the skies are ablaze with splendor, and enjoy baseball with apple pie. America is a place where people all over the world want to live. Although America is just a baby, she has been blessed of God more than any other nation in the history of the world.

Why? One of the reasons is because the Bible says, *"Righteousness exalts a nation, but sin is a reproach to any people"* (Prov. 14:34). Righteousness will also exalt a church, a family, a business, a community, or a Christian. God will honor that which is right. The Bible says, *"Seek ye first the kingdom of God and his righteousness, and all these things will be added unto you."* America is *one nation under God,* where the people can worship God as they please. It is a people planted and born to trust in God alone. Our currency helps us to remember that: *In God we trust!*
I believe America is good and great because of her God, her churches, and those godly principles which have kept her safe and strong.

She has been established by indelible landmarks. These are credible, bedrock, and fundamental.

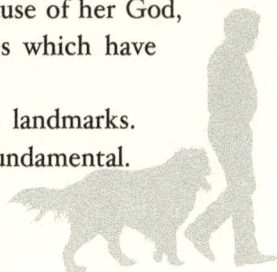

America is a lover of the Bible. Ninety percent of Americans say they believe in the Bible. To believe in the Bible is a Judeo/Christian conviction—a belief in both Old and New Testaments. We believe and will fight for the Ten Commandments to be on display at the town square. These foundational laws of the Bible tell everyone who crosses our borders both who we are and where we are. No other country has an identification such as America. I love this land!

She is busy at work. America is the leader in free enterprise in the world. We can work anywhere. We work and earn our bread by the sweat of our brow. We can buy, sell, invest, and own a piece of these 50 United States. We are a republic, not a socialistic government. America is my land and she is so beautiful!

Indeed, it goes without saying, she is the salt and light of the world. She is the greatest entity through which the Holy Spirit has to work as the restraining force against sin and the devil. The putrefaction of this world has been stopped, slowed, and silenced because of Christians. The message is one: God so loved this world (America is included) that He gave His only Son to die so others can live. America's light of the Gospel is a beacon of hope and a promise of heaven one day. *America, the beautiful!*

—Connect—

This is truly a land where you can...Connect!

JUST A THOUGHT...
Remember President John F. Kennedy:
"And so, my fellow Americans:
Ask not what your country can do for you—
ask what you can do for your country."

Things That Are
Impossible for God

Hebrews 6:17,18

Film actor and movie star, Christopher
Reeve, wrote a book entitled, *Nothing Is Impossible*.
It records a remarkable road to a possible recovery of a spinal
injury that resulted from him falling off a horse seven years ago. It left
him paralyzed from his neck down. Christopher Reeve died on October
10, 2004.

The Bible is clear: With man things are impossible; with God all
things are possible. Anything which leaves God out of the equation
will result in nothing. However, all things are possible when God's will
is a mandate. God can and does use our faith when necessary to move
mountains to be cast into the sea.

God is perfect and complete. He is unchangeable in His power,
attributes, essence, knowledge, and will. He is infinite in truth; there is
no truth apart from him. He is infinite in his holiness; there is no place
for sin to dwell in Him. He is all-powerful; there is no power apart from
Him. He can't think of any way to change. Yet there are things which
are *impossible for God* and for God to do or become.

What God says, He has the power to perform. The Bible says, *It is
impossible for God to lie. Heaven and earth will pass away, but his
words will not pass away*. When He says *all that come unto
me, I will in no wise will cast out,* this is truth. Those who
do come, will in no wise perish. This is His promise.
It is *impossible for God* not to fulfill His will. This
is assurance!

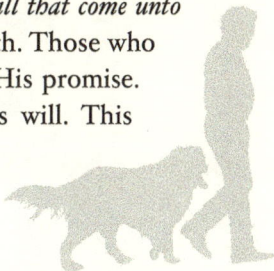

The Bible says, *Whosever shall offend in one point, he is guilty of all* (Jas. 2:10). It is *impossible for God* to look on any sin with any degree of allowance. If one of the Ten Commandments have been broken, one is guilty of them all being broken. Can nine pins on a bowling alley be knocked down and it be called a strike? It is *impossible for God* to tolerate any sin in anyone and that person not feel guilty. It is that guilt which draws us to God by way of repentance, sorrow for sin, and a renewed fellowship with Him.

For God so loved the world, that whosoever believeth in him (God's only begotten Son) should not perish, but have everlasting life (John 3:16). It is *impossible for God* to love some while hating others. God loves all babies and what babies will become when they grow up with an unchanging love. God is love! God loves you and me, and it is *impossible for God* to respond in any other way. He loves a world of people and has proved that unconditional love in the gift of His own Son, Jesus Christ.

— *Connect* —————————

It is impossible for God not to love you and me!

JUST A THOUGHT…
For God to change, it would require Him to become better or worse.

Kidnapping, Killings, and Kids

Matthew 2:18

In Rama there was a voice heard, *lamentation, and weeping, and great mourning,* *Rachel weeping for her children, and would not be comforted, because* *they are not.*

Every day in America, more than 4,000 unborn babies are slaughtered by way of abortion. More unborn babies perish each day than those murdered on 9-11! Before midnight tonight, 28,000 unborn babies will be murdered. Studies show over 50,000 children will come up missing this year. Our kids today do not have a safe playground, some are not even safe at night in their own bedrooms.

A wicked, murderous King Herod killing two-year-olds, sending a blood-chilling terror of any worst nightmare to mothers—still lives in the 21st century.

This fear riveted our own back yard, when Kristin Jackson, a 14-year-old teenager, was kidnapped at the Wayne County Fair. She was missing for several days, until dismembered parts of her body were found. Both Mr. and Mrs. Jackson have been surrounded by a host of loving people in the community. Their weeping, sorrow, and great mourning has been like a shot heard around the world coming from a little "sleepy town" like Wooster, Ohio.

The ultimate blame for this needless news rests with Satan; he is the reason for this heartache. There is coming for him one day a higher court, and there will be no appeal. The judge of all the earth will slam him into the everlasting lake of fire. Until that time, we

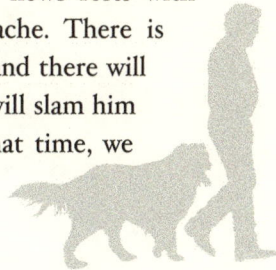

live in a very cruel, sinful, and horrible world. It has been cursed with evil imaginations from wicked hearts who know no depths to which they can sink. Man is totally depraved; there is not one good, no not one. When deranged minds fall into the will of the devil, there will be kidnappings and killings, and our kids will not be coming home.

Dr. James Dobson (Focus on the Family) recently blamed these occurrences on pornography—the evolution of which develops into the most heinous crimes. Child pornography can ultimately lead to child-murders. America today needs to go to the polls and vote *King Herod* out of office. However, today we have a man of God in office (President Bush) who desires to stop this brutal accepted agenda against the unborn.

The structure of the home has a role in the killings of our kids. Mr. and Mrs. Van Dam, whose thrills of drugs and spouse-swapping have much to answer to their little girl who was snatched from her bedroom, raped, and murdered. When our homes become the playboy way of life, our kids will be kidnapped and killed!

— *Connect* —

Gather your children around an old-fashioned altar in your home and pray with them and for them...by name and by need.

JUST A THOUGHT...
*It is not the will of the heavenly Father
that one of these little ones perish.*

Bah, Humbug!
Matthew 2:11

When they had opened their treasures, they presented unto him gifts; gold, and frankincense, and myrrh.

The *"scrooge"* of Christmas lives on. They say...it's pagan and a happy day for the marketplace. It has no meaning, it's commercialism, and a wasted day in the workforce. Bah, humbug!

Is there any rhyme or reason why during the most wonderful time of the year people all over the world travel to come home for family, bearing good and great gifts, enjoying the lights, trees, decorations, homemade candy, and all the food? The answer is "yes" and without any hesitation. It is Christmas, for crying out loud! It only happens this way once a year—it is a time of great rejoicing of receiving and sharing gifts with each other. We do this because of Jesus' birthday.

Several things come to my mind. One and foremost is, God chose to start all of this by the giving of His Son as a baby born in Bethlehem. No gift has ever been equaled or appreciated more. Whatever happens to all men who have ever been born will be the result of this one gift. Life here and there will be determined because of JESUS, God's Son, and what we will do with Him. We who have received Him, now can give Him to others and make Christmas happen daily. You will never appreciate a gift till you receive it (Him).

Another thing that comes as I muse over the gifts that the wise men gave to Jesus on His birthday (*gold, frankincense, and myrrh*). How much was given by these wise men and how much did Mary and Joseph receive on behalf of Baby Jesus is determined on how many wise men there

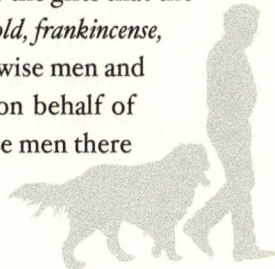

were. Many scholars of the world believe there were more than three wise men—maybe like 300 or so! Wow—300 wise men bringing all that good stuff! There was a big Christmas on that day! Did Mary and Joseph say, *"Now, guys, this is Jesus' birthday; all this traveling and gifts is foolishness. "Bah, humbug!"* Are you kidding me?! They took the gifts with great joy and appreciation. Just a note here: This poor family would need such gifts to get them to Egypt later when the *"grinch"* of Christmas (Herod) would go on a rampage of murdering all the children that were two years of age and under. Come on, and give a big gift, others will take it and enjoy it! When you give a gift this year, see that it is a gift God can use in someone's life.

And another thing...! We learn to give good and precious gifts by following the example of God. God loved this world so much, that He gave His only begotten Son. We spare no expense within our means and budget during this time of the year. Paul quoted our Lord one time by saying, *"It is more blessed to give than to receive."* I want to say to the *"scrooges," "grinches,"* and *"bah-humbuggers"*: Christ died for you too and wants you to have the peace that passes all understanding—peace that is so rare, needed, and precious in this day of war. It is because of Jesus that we have peace; you can't take that away from me.

A Merry Christmas to the *"humbuggers"* everywhere. You have added the "Season's Greetings" and "Happy Holidays" to replace Merry Christmas! Christ is still in Christmas and remains the reason for the season.

—Connect—

Give Jesus to someone today; it is the most expensive gift you can give...and He is free!

JUST A THOUGHT...
If Herod had it to do all over again, he would not have tried to destroy Jesus, and neither should you.

What Will Seeing Jesus Face to Face Be Like

Revelation 22:4

Jim Hill wrote the world a song from God:
"What a day that will be, when my Jesus I shall see, and I look upon His face, the one who saved me by His grace." These words make us want to say as the Greeks: *"Sirs, we would see Jesus."*

No one living in this world today knows what Jesus looked like. Yet, when you get to heaven, no one will have to be introduced to Him. When you see Him, you will know Him. Seeing Jesus face to face on that day will be as if you were standing in a mirror, a full revelation of all that Jesus is will suddenly appear visibly before your eyes. All surroundings will be secondary and all fears will pass. Our words will be (if any) as those of Thomas: *"My Lord and my God!"*

There is no part of the body that is more revealing than the face. It makes up about nine square inches and there are not two of us that look exactly alike. The face becomes a window of all that lies within. Any fears, anxieties, hurts, frustrations, sadness, happiness, hostility, or dejections can suddenly appear on this small area of our flesh. With each face comes a name which only fits the face. The face of Jesus bears His name: one of love, grace, mercy, and peace.

Seeing Jesus face to face will be as if you were standing in the very presence of God. Philip said to Jesus, *"Show us the Father."* Jesus said, *"Philip, when you see me, you have seen the Father."* Being in the presence of God will cause the mighty to fall to the ground in humbleness, reverence,

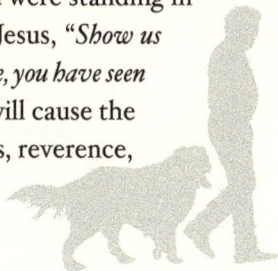

and in true worship. This is what it will be like when you see Jesus face to face.

What else remains to be seen with any desire after seeing Jesus face to face? There is nothing beyond; all becomes just a backdrop that gives way to this prominent person, God's only Son. It will be a perfect day, no darkness ever will faintly dim the day, and the light of Jesus will cast all shadows forever away.

He is the Promised Land. He flows with milk and honey without price. He is the bread from heaven and the water of life. He is the door and He has the keys of life and death. All the promises of the Bible are summed up in one name, one word: JESUS! Seeing JESUS face to face is assurance, peace, and fulfillment.

Seeing Jesus face to face will cause all former images of Him to pass away. There will be no more cuts, bruises, black eyes, bloodstained blotches, and no more cries of being forsaken. When you turn your eyes upon Jesus and look full into His wonderful face...things of earth will grow strangely dim, in the light of His glory and grace.

— *Connect* —

"Face to face with Christ my Savior. Face to face, what will it be? When with rapture I behold him, Jesus Christ who died for me!"

J UST A THOUGHT...
When time changes into eternity, whose face will you see?

The Holy Spirit—
His Personal Work
John 15:26,27

But when the Comforter is come, whom I will send unto you from the Father, even the Spirit of truth, which proceedeth from the Father, he shall testify of me: And ye also shall bear witness, because ye have been with me from the beginning.

The *Holy Spirit*—the co-equal of God and Jesus Christ, is a *"People Person"* with a *"personal touch."* He is the personal missionary, the evangelist, and the pastor that can stand and assist every believer in this world. He can encourage, empower, and will equip the child of God to do and be all that God has intended for him to be. He is not an "Energizing Bunny," He is all-powerful, all-knowing, and present everywhere at the same time in our lives. A God-given special assistant to enable any to live godly in a sin-cursed world.

Jesus called Him the *"Comforter,"* the one who will take every step with us. Close enough to talk, listen, care, lead, guide, guard, and be our companionship. He not only knows, but He cares. He is moved at our feelings, and with compassion He heals the hurt. He is grieved as well when we walk contrary to His will. When He corrects, it will always be the truth. His truth will rebuke and repair. He is kind, gentle, but firm in His admonition. This Comforter is too wise to leave us in error and fault. He is too loving to leave us the way we want to be. And He is too honest not to tell us the truth.

From the creation of this world to the cremation of this world, He has always been. He is God the Holy Spirit; there has not been a time when He was not. *"In the beginning was the Word..."* As God, He was before all things as He is before you and me. Were He not there before us, we would not be aware where He is, nor would we be aware where we would be. His love and convicting power to expose our sin and the Savior of the world into our lives is to bring us to a place of repentance. This is the personal work which He loves to do!

Jesus said He would send Him unto us, developing a personal relationship which would never end. This coming would be a permanent indwelling, the taking up of a residence inside each of us who responds to the call of God. His presence will seal us, fill us, preserve us, equip us, protect us, and give us power to witness. He always shows up for work in the workplace to accomplish the will of the Father.

He will never leave His *"first love,"* which is to personally testify of Jesus Christ and His purpose as the Son of God. He will point out that Jesus was born of a virgin, but was born to die. Not just to die, but to die for the judgment of all men. He will emphasize that Jesus became our Mediator as He met the righteous demands of God. He will point out the fact of the sacrifice for sin and the price for sin. He will be direct and to the point that Jesus is the only begotten Son of God, full of grace and truth. The Holy Spirit will exalt Him up on the cross as well as on the throne. He will preach that Jesus is the Savior of the world, the judge of all sinners, and the King of kings. This He will do until the church, the body of Christ, is called home. This is His personal work!

Connect

Let the Holy Spirit do what He came to do in your life today.

JUST A THOUGHT...
The Holy Spirit will speak this truth at any expense.

Fainting in the
Day of Adversity
Proverbs 24:10

If thou faint in the day of adversity, thy strength is small (Proverbs 25:10).

Never has there been a man born that has not been born into trouble. *Man that is born of woman is of few days and full of trouble.* Men are not "gods," men born of the flesh remain flesh, a human nature which is totally depraved. There can be nothing good found in a wicked heart. There is not a man born of women which has not been cumbered about with much fear.

A fainting spirit is a concern we all have, and it is one which must be faced with solid principles from a strong faith in the Word of God. *He that doeth the will of God will abide forever.* Everyone will sooner or later face "the perfect storm" in life. A storm which will overflow the bows with despondency and care. At which time in life one finds himself totally helpless, and somewhat hopeless, in which the best of our strength becomes worthless. However, there are life preservers and lifeboats which we can flee to when suddenly we are in the midst of a storm, when all hope is removed that we might be saved.

Crises of life are like tempest waves of the sea. They keep coming one right after another. Somewhere along the shores of a storm, you will find a lighthouse, a beacon in the darkest hour. That one is Christ, your Lord and Savior. He is positioned upon a rock which has withstood the fury and the pressure from the gates of hell. He has

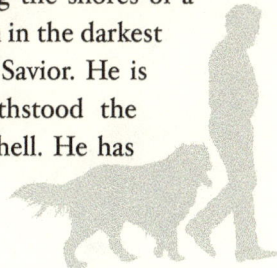

promised that He would never leave you nor forsake you—look for Him in your day of adversity, though your strength may be small, and you will find Him. A true unfailing light which will see you through any storm. You will find the strength to face any barbs from coming from the one who seeks to destroy you.

Depression is a horrible problem to encounter. It is a low ebb, and we feel like throwing all overboard into the depths of the sea. You have rowed and exhausted all your strength, the winds have taken away your trust, and your heart which was once filled with praise has turned to murmuring and complaints. You begin to faint in the day of adversity. Remember this, *"Greater is he that is in you, than he which is in the world."* Grace brings a new refreshing moment that will fill your sails to a new direction. God's grace has been measured for you.

When facing these times, remember, there are others who are hanging by a thread depending on you to make it. They are watching us as if we were actors on a stage. We must perform, and we must perform at our best. Some will come to trust Christ as their Savior when they see the perseverance of the saints. The Bible will become a source of strength as they see you live it to the letter and through it to the latter. And this will silence the scoffers when they see you coming into the dock as a testimony of God's deliverance.

— *Connect* —

Stay in the boat; the shore is just ahead; you are going to make it!

JUST A THOUGHT...
Many have given up just at the break of the day.

A Double-Minded Man

James 1:8

Remember...Jennifer Wilbanks, age 32, the *"Runaway Bride"?* After a concocted story of being kidnapped by abductors, a coast-to-coast manhunt, and a family that was ripped into leaving a seemingly gaping hole, Jennifer then returned to her home in Duluth, Georgia. Just one week before a wedding of 600 guests, fourteen bridesmaids and groomsmen, and to her fiancé, John Mason, she got *"cold feet"* and *"just had to get away!"* The best we can say with the information we now have is what Pastor Jones said, *"Jennifer is alive and we are thankful for that!"*

We live in a day when nothing seems to be fixed with any surety or longevity. People are on the move—moving to another state, another job, another wife or husband, and another "god." Doubled-mindedness is accepted as quality and virtue in this new millennium. Their resumé is endless where they have been and what they have done.

God is looking for husbands and wives to stand in the gap. Stand and keep standing for a cause and purpose until we are called home one day to meet the Lord and to receive a full reward. A doubled-minded person does not know how to *"occupy till he comes."*

Commitment to a wife or a husband is until death do us part, not till we tear each other apart. Our God is a God of forgiveness and one who gives the second chance. Like David who will always have the sword of judgment hanging over his head, Jennifer Wilbanks will always be seen walking through the airport with a blanket covering her embarrassing return. The wound she has left can be healed, but not without a scar.

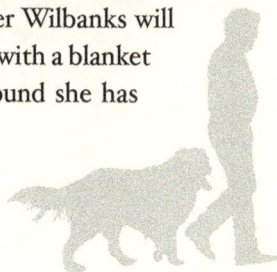

Marriage is an act of constantly leaving and cleaving. God said, man will leave his mother and father and cleave unto his wife. Interesting, the meaning of word *cleave* is the same word as the word leprosy! It is a word which means being stuck with or being glued to. When marriage takes place it is like being glued together, like a leprosy has developed! The vows between a man and a woman are like the commandments of God, *they are not grievous,* but easy and enjoyable. A doubled-minded man in marriage will take his hand off the plough and will always look back. *Remember Lot's wife!*

A doubled-minded man is unstable in all his ways. A doubled-minded man is never grounded in faith. He is as a bobber being tossed around in a shoreless sea and without a lifeline. That man will never have any footing, no direction in his life, and will always live in fear. The problem is, there is just no place to...*get away.* He or she will be like a staggering drunk, always being between the devil and the deep blue sea.

The question has been asked, "Will John Mason give Jennifer a second chance?" I hope so. A bad situation is better than a broken one, and a bad marriage is better than a broken marriage. God can indeed give grace to any side that bears any thorns. Marriage that is honorable can be tolerable and enjoyable.

— *Connect* —

How does one remedy doubled-mindedness? By having the singleness of the mind of Christ. Let this mind be in you. Faith is the substance of things hoped for, the evidence of things not seen.

JUST A THOUGHT...
I wonder what Jennifer would do if she had it to do all over again.

Does This Offend You?

John 6:61

Amazing as it sounds, yet after the miracle of feeding about 5,000 men (maybe 20,000 with women and children) with five loaves and two fish, there was a mass exodus when Jesus said that real life can be only found in Him (John 6:53-58). Jesus is without question, *"The Bread of Life."* He not only can feed 20,000, but He can feed the world! By accepting the sacrifice of His body and blood from the cross and taking Him into your life by faith, any person can have life, and life abundantly.

When this crowd heard this, they became confused and walked back into a life filled with turmoil and emptiness. They wanted their belly filled but did not want Jesus in their heart. Like today, many do not want this way to real life. Ted Turner said, *"It is foolish to think that Jesus Christ is the only way to heaven!"* He like these having been fed with loaves and fishes becomes offended! *Blessed is he that is not offended in me.*

There is a fundamental principle of all of the teachings of Jesus—which is, He would never say anything to hurt or offend anyone. He is too kind, wise, and loving to hurt any of the little ones. He said, *"It would be better for a man to have never been born than to hurt a little child."* Anything we hear from our Lord will be only for our good and for God's glory.

Is it offensive that Jesus is all He claimed to be? Jesus being God the Son is not received by all. Yet there are those of us like Peter, who will say very confidently, *"Thou art the Christ, the Son of the living God."* Peter, a Jew, said something like this, "I believe you are the Messiah promised from the Old Testament. And you are indeed all that you claim to be!" What a mouthful! Does that offend you?

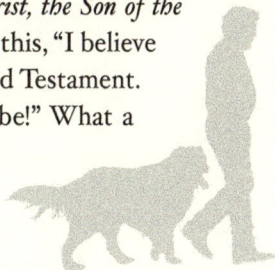

Does it offend any when Jesus says, *"I am the bread of life?"* He told this multitude that Moses gave bread which had to be gathered up day after day. By the *"Bread of Life,"* Jesus was saying, "I am the only Bread from heaven who can satisfy and fill completely." When He said, *"I am the life,"* He was saying, "Besides me there is no other life." Does that offend any?

Does it offend any when Jesus searches your heart and brings up the *sin which so easily besets us?* Someone has carefully said, *"There is a sin in all of our lives which can take us down any moment."* From time to time, Jesus will bring it up, lay it on the table, and ask, "When are you going to do something about this?" These are *hard sayings* of Jesus (60). Make no mistake about this, He will be totally honest with you all the time.

— Connect —

Allow Him and His words be all that He claims
to be in your life and live!

JUST A THOUGHT...
If Jesus has not said anything hard to you,
He probably has never said anything to you!

Coals of Fire On
Your Enemy's Head
Proverbs 25:21,22

If thine enemy be hungry, give him bread to eat; and if he be thirsty, give him water to drink: For thou shalt heap coals of fire upon his head, and the LORD shall reward thee (Proverbs 25:21,22).

Our head tells us to render fire for fire when our enemies have done evil to us. To get even or to get back at that person is the fair and right thing to do. Do unto others what they have done to us; do it more than what they have done unto us and with good measure. When we do so, it will teach them a good lesson to never do that to us again. However, our heart tells us we are the children of God, we are not of this world, and neither should we respond as the world does. Christians turn the other cheek.

Paul strengthens this: *Therefore if thine enemy hunger, feed him; if he thirst, give him drink: for in so doing thou shalt heap coals of fire on his head. Be not overcome of evil, but overcome evil with good* (Rom. 12:20,21).

Heaping coals of fire upon the enemies' head wins the war with our enemies. Our objective is never to hurt as we have been hurt, but to reconcile, restore, and to redeem. In doing so, we can win our neighbor. We are to forgive and to forget as we have been forgiven by our heavenly Father. Keep in mind the story of Joseph and his brethren. Joseph overcame evil with good for the good of his enemies.

Loving those who hate us is a burning ember that will leave a lasting mark upon another which will

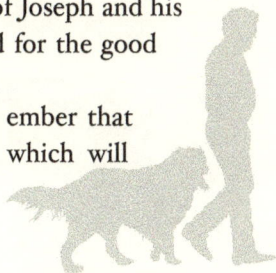

never be forgotten. When we love those who love us, what reward do we have? But when we love those like our heavenly Father loved those who crucified His Son, we see them not who or what they are, but what they can be. Loving an Onesimus makes a choice servant. Love covers a multitude of sins.

Forgiving is coal which never cools down. Have you ever said this to those who have wronged you as though they had just nailed you to a cross: *"Father, forgive them, for they know not what they do"*? When they see and hear this, it makes an indelible impression upon them. It will annihilate any issue to ashes. Jacob and Esau did this. Why can't their cousins today do the same? *Blessed are the peacemakers!*

Behaving like children of the Father keeps a relationship from growing cold. We can never expect any good coming from our enemy, but any good that comes to our enemy will come from the Father. Jesus heaped coals of fire with His acts of kindness, forgiveness, and doing the Father's will in the volume of the book written of Him. We who were once enemies of the Father have now been tempered, molded, and fashioned in His likeness under the fires of His compassion.

— Connect

Find someone who needs a change of heart, soul, and spirit,
apply the heat, and enjoy the transformation.

JUST A THOUGHT...
The best thing that can happen to our enemy
is for our enemy to become our friend.

Revival in Our Time
Habakkuk 3:2

O LORD, revive thy work in the midst
of the years, in the midst of the years make known...

Our shelves are filled with books whose authors have written about how God moved in their day in great revivals. Men like George Whitfield, Charles Finney, J. Wilbur Chapman, Sam Jones, Billy Sunday, R.A. Torrey, George Truett, Wesley, Vance Havner, and even Billy Graham. These men were men just like us today, but they sought nothing but the power of God as they stood to preach. When Jonathan Edwards preached his famous sermon, "Sinners in the hands of an angry God," it said that men and women stood clutching the backs of the pews until their knuckles turned white, fearing only the God of love and judgment.

Revival can happen today. It must happen if we are to see America saved from internal destruction. It is our only hope for survival. Suicide is an all-time high among teenagers, kids are murderers today and being tried like adults, premarital sex is commonplace among young people, drugs, pornography, homosexuality have become a norm among us, kids know nothing about prayer in the home anymore, and preachers are watering down the Word of God that brings conviction in our churches today. Sin is found today from the White House to Our House.

Revival will come in our day in the midst of all that the lowlife can muster. It will happen when the people of God will seek after Him only with all heart, mind, body, and soul. In our day could be the greatest days of revivals— no other time ever had what we have today. Printed

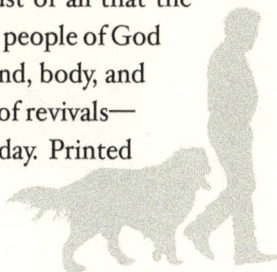

page, TV, colleges and seminaries, Christian schools, great churches, and great preachers. *If my people, which are called by my name, shall humble themselves, and pray, and seek my face, and turn from their wicked ways, then will I (GOD) hear from heaven, and will forgive their sin, and will heal their land.*

We are God's people for this day. We have come to His kingdom for such a time as this. We must have revival in our day for a legacy to those who will follow us to the third and fourth generation.

Connect

*Evangelist Gypsy Smith drew a circle on the ground
and asked God to send a revival inside that circle.
He then stepped into that circle!*

JUST A THOUGHT...

*What will the next generation read
about our time of revival?*

The Strategy of Satan

John 10:10

The thief cometh not, but to steal, and to kill and to destroy...

Mark it down; Satan is the enemy of God and ours too! He is not our friend, no matter how tempting and sensible he makes things to appear. Remember the fruit that fell into the hands of Adam and Eve, but they fell into the hands of Satan and that became the downfall of the human race.

The thief cometh not, but to steal, and to kill, and to destroy... He is in a constant warfare to annihilate the eternal creation of God! This is his game plan, he knows his time is short, and there is no resting with him. The *strategy of Satan* is to take everyone to hell that he can get to believe his lies.

Be not deceived, Satan will come in sheep's clothing. Inside he is a madman, a wolf that has no mercy, a bloodthirsty monster who will take no prisoners.

He has come to destroy man. He wants nothing but all men and all that men have. Satan said to God about Job, *"Let me have him and he will curse your face."* The *strategy of Satan* is to get men to deny God from having any control over their lives. He wants the worship that men give to God.

He has come to stop Christ. He started in the Garden of Eden to destroy man's seed with sin, but God intervened and covered man's sin with blood. He has tried to slaughter the Jews through whom Christ would come; however, Jesus was born in Bethlehem of Judea. He

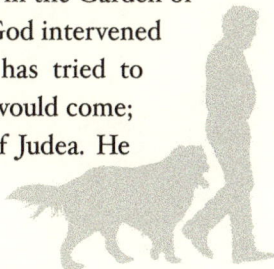

tried to stop Christ at the cross, but here his head was crushed by a bruised heel!

He has come to destroy the Bible. Yet today after thousands of years, the Bible still remains the best seller of any book. God's book is the Bible, it is indestructible, and it will remain when Satan, his critics, and the world pass away.

He has come to try to stop the church. For years there have been false doctrines, false teachers, sin in the church, churches splitting—but, friend, she stands today with the doors open and the lights are on. And yet there is room for more to come.

— *Connect* —————————

Be on the lookout, Satan will come as an angel of light.
Once he has you, he will turn off the switch.

JUST A THOUGHT...
   Satan is your enemy; resist him!

Seven Things Which God Hates

Proverbs 6:16-19

The Bible says that God is love, and indeed He is. It is also true that God hates certain things. He hates those things which make us so much unlike Him. The father who just watched his son stumbling drunk into his house hates the booze that made him do that wicked thing. The old Pentecostal preacher once said, *"Sin will take you where you did not intend to go and will keep you there longer than you intended to stay. At last you are not fit to return home to your family."*

God hates a proud look—eyes which tell one he is a little better than someone else. This proud look caused at least one third of the holy angels who followed Lucifer to be cast out of heaven. Pride goes before a fall. Humble yourselves under the mighty hand of God.

God hates a lying tongue—the littlest member of the human body which is set full of fire from hell. All evil is from the heart which is channeled through the tongue. One does not need his mouth washed out with soap, but a new heart which only God can give.

God hates hands which shed innocent blood—murder! Abortion is at the top of this list with God. Better that a millstone be hanged about a man's neck and he be cast into the sea than to hurt a little one (the unborn)!

God hates a heart that deviseth wicked imaginations—this generation is a wicked and adulterous one. The root of the homosexual agenda today is to move the Creator into the creature, to de-throne God and defy self. God will give this heart up and over to a reprobate mind. God hates this sin!

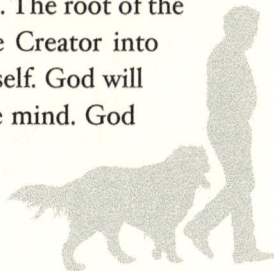

God hates feet which are swift in running to mischief—placing agendas into place for harm. The Oklahoma Federal Building was bombed and many were killed because of the McVeighs and others like him. *"Provide not for the flesh."*

God hates false witnesses—liars, enough said about this one!

God hates the discord which is sown among the brethren—troublemakers. If the Bible is true about *"Blessed are the peacemakers,"* then those who are troublemakers will be cursed. *How good and pleasant it is for brethren to dwell together in unity!*

— *Connect* —

Seven is the number of completion...
God hates all sin, and so should we.

JUST A THOUGHT...

If we love God with all of our heart
we will hate sin with all of our heart.

Two Thieves
Luke 23:32,33

And there were also two other, malefactors, led with him to be put to death. ...one on the right hand, and the other on the left.

The sinless Son of God hanging on a cross between two malefactors—shocking! Another place calls them thieves. They were the vilest of criminals, wicked, perverted, and immoral. The Bible says, as Jesus was being led to Calvary (the place of the skull), these two evil-working culprits were being led to be crucified along with Jesus. The cross of Calvary was a bitter end for a wasted life. These two thieves deserved to be there—but that other man, the one in the middle did nothing amiss. Read this riveting narrative from Luke 23:32-43.

From this passage it is clear that life, as precious as it, is can be wasted in its entirety. *What shall it profit a man, if he shall gain the whole world and lose his own soul?* These two thieves were empty without Christ. These also will come to the end of the day having laid up no treasure. *He that finds his life will lose it, and he that loses his life for my sake, will find it.*

Salvation can be obtained even on a deathbed. This is getting saved at 11:30 P.M.! One of the criminals confessed to Christ that he was a sinner and asked to be remembered. This is indeed the sinner's prayer at the midnight hour. Jesus will save any person, anytime, anywhere from the sin which will damn all men. It is not the sins of the flesh that will send a person to hell, but the sin of un-belief. This one malefactor believed on Christ, was saved, and went to heaven that very day. Glory to God for His amazing grace—grace which is greater than all

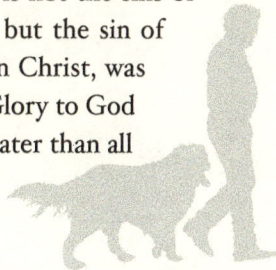

our sin. Just do it now, and have forgiveness the rest of your life, even if it is only for one hour!

All have sinned and come short of the glory of God. We have all missed the mark and have transgressed against His standards. These two thieves were on either side of the suffering Savior. All mankind is either on the right or the left of Him. I would like to think that the believing sinner was on the right! And the unbelieving sinner was on the left. All are either for Him or against Him. He is either our Master or the one mocked and made fun of. It appears that for a period of time from the other account of the Gospels that both of these thieves railed on Jesus. But the one who watched Him for some of those six long hours believed—he now is *right* with His Lord.

The sweetest words ever spoken by Jesus were: *"Father, forgive them, for they know not what they do."* God takes no pleasure in the death of the wicked and gives all men space to repent. *He is not willing that any should perish, but that all come to repentance.* I wait to hear of this dying thief in heaven one day.

— Connect

"Wasted years, wasted years, oh how foolish!"

J UST A THOUGHT...
  Today is the day of salvation; now is the accepted time.

"Be Still and Know That I Am God"

Psalm 46:10

Be still, and know that I am God: I will be exalted among the heathen, I will be exalted in the earth.

President George W. Bush concluded his historic address before Congress, the nation, and the world by saying, *"In all that lies before us, may God grant us wisdom, and may He watch over the United States of America."*

Be still, and know that I am God. Hush, not a word; be still, hold your peace, and rest in confidence that I am God. God is saying to us, "What I am doing, you do not know now, but later you will understand." God is saying to America, *"I will be exalted among the heathen and the earth!"*

Tuesday, September 11, 2001, was a day when America and people all over the world were called on by God to pray. Things happened in which we could do nothing at the time but to call upon God to help us. He is indeed *"our refuge and strength, a very present help in a time of trouble."* We found support from different people from different faiths as we knelt together in homes, churches, workplace, school yards, Congress, and many other places. The Bible says, *"If my people, which are called by my name, will pray, and seek my face, and turn from their wicked ways, then will I hear from heaven, and will forgive their sin, and will heal their land."* Be still—God has heard us!

God is watching over America because of who she is. She is *"one nation under God."* She is a land born in freedom—freedom to worship. She is a land which

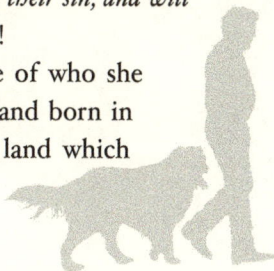

allows us to worship God freely in spirit and in truth. We do not have some dictator regulating our church services. We are able to preach, baptize our converts, ordain them, and send them out into the world for evangelization. What God has given to America is become the hope to many third-world countries. Needless to say, God is indeed watching over us. We have learned in these days who God is!

God loves America, as He loves all people all over this world. In America, we have the freedom of speech and the press. When we raise and wave the flag, it's the greatest flag anywhere, and the world knows it. It's *Old Glory*, it's the red, white, and blue. America is patriotic and not ashamed of it. This flag stands for *life, liberty, and the pursuit of happiness*. Many have died for it to remain raised. When reminded of the fallen she flies half-staffed in memory of all who have lost their lives under the attack of terrorism. Yet she is seen everywhere in America. Yes, God is watching over America. In our hearts, there is a peace which passes all understanding in knowing that His ears are open to our cry and His eyes neither slumber nor sleep.

In complete confidence we know there is a God who is above all gods. He is the true and holy God of the Holy Bible. His Son is Jesus Christ, the Savior of the world. Our faith is in Him, the only true God.

— *Connect* —

We learn in times of adversities just who God is.

J U S T   A   T H O U G H T…
Shh!— we are in His presence!

Male and Female

Genesis 1:27

So God created man in his own image, in the image of God created he him; male and female created he them.

God created man from the dust of the ground, and then He made Eve from one of Adam's ribs. He placed them in the Garden of Eden to enjoy each other, the new world, and the company of Himself. The apex of God's creation is that of male and female.

This distinction of "male and female" has been a divisive line from the beginning. Sides have developed, opinions have been adopted, and battles have been fought over the way God had first ordained this union. There are those who have said they don't like the way God did it, which results in those who are defending the way God did it. To one crowd, gender is given, to another gender is changeable.

Male and female is the only way for a healthy monogamous relationship. It was not good for man to be alone, so God created a helpmeet for him. She would be the fulfillment of all that man needed. He would be the safety and security blanket for all the woman needed. Each are driven with separate and unique desires which could only be satisfied by each other. Even today, *man will leave his father and mother and cleave unto his wife.* Ever since the creation of Adam and Eve, male and female have been attracted to each other and drawn naturally to each other in a wholesome relationship.

Male and female is God's way of extending the home. Procreation was God's way of expanding this relationship. Only male and female can produce a child

which is honorable. One man for one woman, and that for a lifetime. God would use this relationship to carry His truth to the third and fourth generation. For male and female to cease and become male and male or female and female would bring us to a *terminal generation*.

Male and female stereotypes the church. An exclusive union of married man and woman is likened unto the church of Jesus Christ. Christ and His bride (the church) is the most beautiful teaching of the Bible. Christ loved the church and gave His life for it. All those who have sinned now can have their robes washed and made white in the blood of the Lamb, being made ready for the Marriage Supper of Christ and His church. Male and female, these two are one. Anything else but this analogy is spoil, putrefaction, and hellish.

—— *Connect* ————

Give thanks for your father and mother for their coming together as one; otherwise you would not be here!

JUST A THOUGHT…
Male and female, it is only natural.

My Only Regret as a Christian

Nevertheless I am continually with thee: thou hast holden me by my right hand. Thou shalt guide me with thy counsel, and afterward receive me to glory. Whom have I in heaven but thee? and there is none upon earth that I desire beside thee (Psalm 73:23-25).

My brand-new life started for me during a 1955 Friday night Fall Revival, as I knelt at an old mourner's bench in a little Nazarene Church in Coal Grove, Ohio, at the age of twelve. I remember the night as if it were last night, when my sister Garnet prayed with me and told me to trust and accept Christ to be my personal Savior by faith. I did!

On May 18, 1963, Jeanie and I (childhood sweethearts) married and soon began a Christian home, serving the Lord as members at the Ice Creek Missionary Baptist Church in Deering, Ohio. We worked as youth workers and Sunday School teachers until the call came to my life to serve the Lord in the ministry. It was in 1968 at a youth camp that I knew for sure of God's call upon my life, to which I yielded unto the Lord as to His direction in His will.

In the summer of 1972, Jeanie and I and our two boys sold out and headed to Lynchburg, Virgina, where Dr. Jerry Falwell and the Thomas Road Baptist Church had started a brand-new college: The Lynchburg Baptist College. Jeanie and I enrolled in college and our two sons (Brett and Todd) enrolled in the Christian Academy.

Upon graduation in 1975, we went to Ironton, Ohio, to start a brand-new church: The Gateway Baptist Church. The call to the pastorate took us to Bible Baptist Church in Jacksonville, Florida, in 1985, and then in 1987 to the Northside Baptist Church in Millersburg, Ohio. During

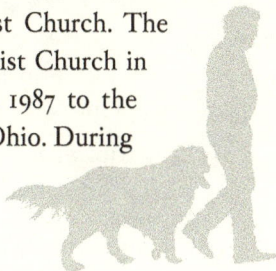

these years both Brett and Todd graduated from Liberty University and married Christian wives from that same university.

Brett and Tatiana are parents of Madison and Taylor. God has blessed their Christian home, the children are saved, they are serving God as a family, and are blessed with a Christian business. Todd and Sue are parents of Cara and Nathan. They are also blessed with a Christian home and the children are saved. They are serving in the full-time pastorate.

Jeanie and I are now in our fourth quarter of our marriage and ministry and enjoy seeing God answering our prayers every day which were prayed more than 40 years ago. His blessings are now into the third generation in our ministry and with our family.

With His continued presence, I have found the absence of fear, perfect peace, unlimited provision, constant protection, joy unspeakable, sufficient grace, undeserved mercy, unconditional love, thrill of victory, unusual strength, eternal hope, divine wisdom, ever-present help in time of trouble, complete forgiveness, wise counsel, tender care, endearing patience, gentle nurturing, and the promises of heaven one day. Hedged by the providence of His will and guided by His wise counsel, He will guide me all the way to glory. I now await till death's departure or that day like unto Enoch and Elijah in which I will be translated and be caught up to be with Him in grandeur of that blissful state of the redeemed forever and ever. Because there is none like unto Him in this life or in that life to come, I have been abundantly blessed.

God leads His dear children along.

In shady, green pastures, so rich and so sweet, Where the water's cool flow bathes the weary one's feet, Sometimes on the mount where the sun shines so bright, Sometimes in the valley, in darkest of night, Though sorrows befall us and evils oppose, Through grace we can conquer, defeat all our foes, Away from the mire, and away from the clay, Away up in glory, eternity's day, Some through the waters, some through the flood, Some through the fire, but all through the blood; Some through great sorrow, but God gives a song, In the night season and all the day long. God leads His dear children along (Young).

My only regret as a Christian is...that I did not give my life over to Him much earlier than I did, rendering unto the Lord and love of my life a great service. What a trip, what a journey, what a family, what a great God and Savior, and what a future that lies just straight ahead for me.

Connect

Ask God what He would have you to do.

J UST A THOUGHT…

Do you have a story to tell?

I Love My Master

Exodus 21:5

I love my master, my wife, and my children; *I will not go out free.*

You've got to read this story from Exodus 21:2-6, concerning a Hebrew servant. God gave instructions regarding Hebrew slaves (men and women) which were bought by their masters. They were to remain slaves for six years, after which they were given a choice to stay with their master or leave as a free person. Should he choose to remain as a slave, he was taken to the judges (maybe a town square) and there his master would pierce his ear with an awl. It would be an "earmark," a sign to all others for two things: One to remain a slave and two to remain a slave with this master.

He was saying to all who would ever see him: *"I love my master* (5) and I choose to stay a slave for my master the rest of my life." I think this is one of the most remarkable readings of the Scripture that anyone could ever read.

The slave after serving six years had to face a decision either to leave as a free man or stay a slave with this master. Thoughts may have run through his mind somewhat like this: "Before I was purchased by this man, I had no place to call home like I do now. I was never cared for by anyone like my master cares for me. I eat better here as a slave than I have ever eaten before. I have better clothes than I have ever had. I have better company than I have ever known. I know where I have come from, whose I am, and what will happen to me in the future. How can I leave what has been so good to me compared to what I was and

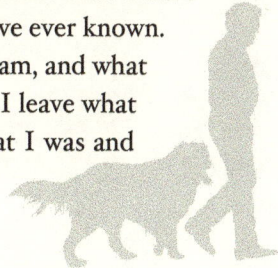

where I could be? I am better off being a slave to my master than to be free in this world. I am going to get my ear pierced!"

If you will permit me to "spiritualize" a little with this text. We as believers are much like these Hebrew slaves. We were sold into sin by one man who yielded unto Satan by transgressing the laws of God. By one man's sin and death by sin, we all are sinners and we will all die. *We have all sinned and come short of the glory of God.*

However, here comes a Master (Christ) who has entered into the slave market, paid the required price (His blood), took us from the bondage of sin, and set us free. We call this the great doctrine of redemption. He has freed us from sin, death, and the grave—this is freedom!

I love my Master, and I am choosing to stay with Him as a servant. He loves me and proved that by dying for me on a cross. He has forgiven me and given me peace. I have the joy of serving Him, loving Him, pleasing Him, and telling others about Him. I am better off now, and when time changes into eternity, He will take me to heaven. I've got to tell you, "*I love my Master!*"

— Connect —

There is a mark upon me which everyone can see,
which is joy unspeakable and full of glory.

JUST A THOUGHT…
Every once in a while, tug on that ear lobe!

The Right Tract

God wants you to be born again:

For God so loved the world that he gave his only begotten
Son that whosoever believes in him should not perish, but
have everlasting life. John 3:16
But God commendeth His love to us in that while we yet
sinners, Christ died for us. Rom. 5:8

To go to heaven, you must be born again:

"Except a man be born again, he can not see or enter the
kingdom of God. You must be born again" John 3:1-7

Why must you be born again:

All have sinned and come short of the glory of God. Rom. 3:23
The wages of sin is death. Rom. 6:23
Whosoever was not found written in the book of life was
cast into the lake of fire. Rev. 20:15

When must you be born again:

I have heard you in an accepted time, now is
the accepted time, now is the day of salvation.
II Cor. 6:2

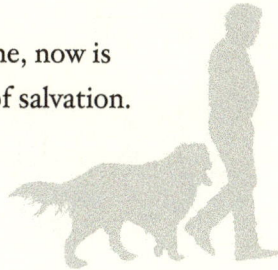

What you must do to be born again:

If you will confess with your mouth the Lord Jesus, and believe in your heart that God hath raised him (Jesus) from the dead, you will be saved. For whosoever shall call upon the name of the Lord shall be saved.
Rom. 10: 9, 13

You can be assured of being born again:

These things have I written unto you that believe on the name of the Son of God: that you may know you have eternal life. I John 5:13
He that hears my word, and believes on him that sent me, hath everlasting life, and shall not come into condemnation; but is passed from death unto life. John 5:24

Pray this prayer to be born again:

God be merciful to me a sinner. I believe Jesus suffered and died for me. Right now I trust in Jesus to be my Savior. I repent of my sin. Take me to Heaven when I die. In Jesus name, Amen.

Time and place when I was born again:

Name _____

Place _____ Time and Date _____

CLIFF HARTLEY
6992 SR 39 Millersburg, Ohio 44654

About the Author

Great stories capture and hold an audience's attention from start to finish. Why should the Gospel message be any different?

In *Saturday Night Musings,* Pastor Cliff Hartley delivers captivating and practical messages that oftentimes draw from current news events. In these clear and concise writings you will find principles for daily living, practical biblical applications, and see into the heart of a local pastor as he feeds his church.

Cliff Hartley, born in Coal Grove, Ohio, has been pastoring for 30 years. He has enjoyed successful ministries in Ironton, Ohio, as a church planter, and in Jacksonville, Florida. For the past eighteen years he has served as Senior Pastor of the Northside Baptist Church in Millersburg, Ohio. This church has grown and matured under his leadership and pastoral care. The insights found in this book are excerpts of the message that he has preached and the Gospel that he loves.

He was saved at twelve years of age and has dedicated his life to learning and loving the Word of God. Cliff received his education at Liberty Baptist College, now Liberty University in Lynchburg, Virginia. He resides in Millersburg, Ohio, with his wife of 43 years, Jeanie Hartley. Their two sons and their wives and four grandchildren also reside in Millersburg, Ohio.